# UNDERSEA WARFARE

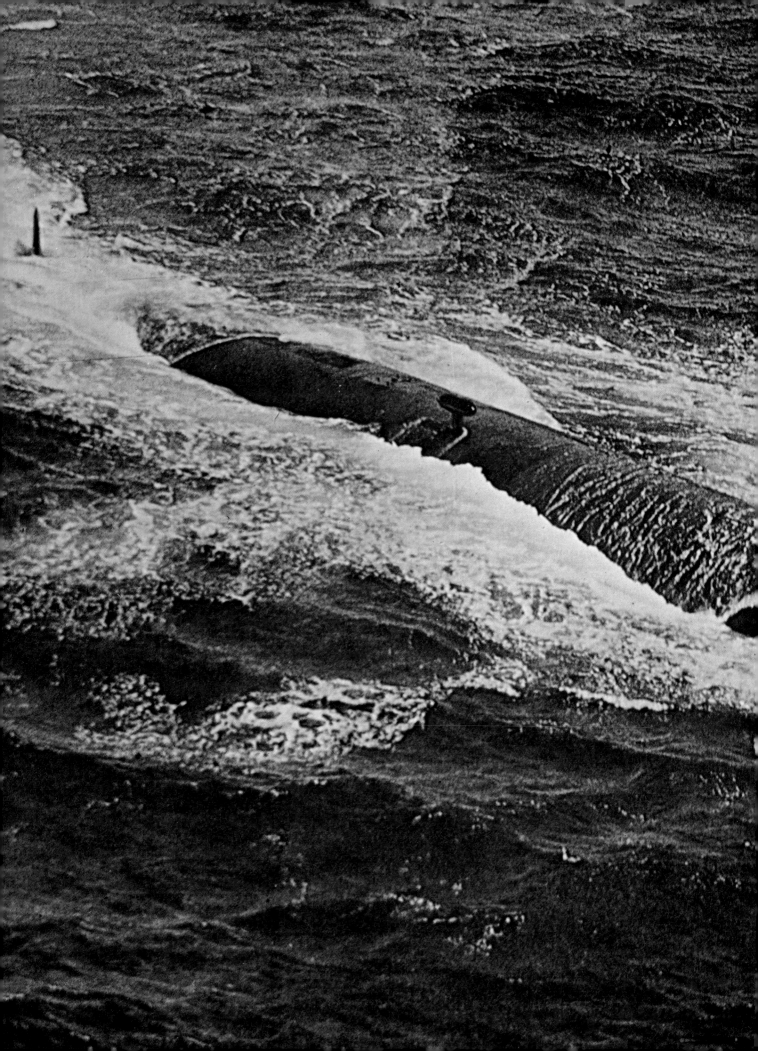

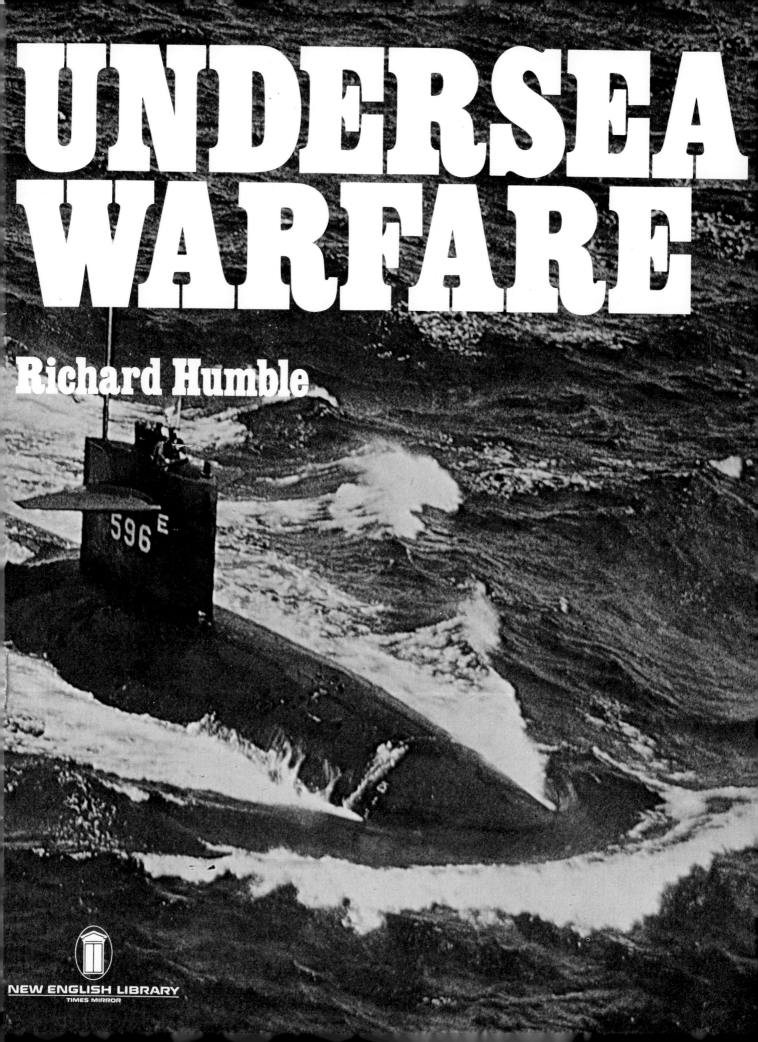

# UNDERSEA WARFARE

## Richard Humble

NEW ENGLISH LIBRARY
TIMES MIRROR

Designed by Roy Williams
Edited by Janet MacLennan
Line Illustrations by Peter Cannings.
Maps by Richard Natkiel
Picture Research by John Moore

ISBN 0 450 04866 7

# CONTENTS

# INTRODUCTION

Three vehicles, perfected since 1900, have revolutionised man's awareness of the limitations of his planet and its insignificance in the Universe: the submarine, the aeroplane, and the rocket spacecraft. Each in turn enables mankind to penetrate beneath the surface of the world's oceans, to traverse its atmosphere, or to reach its neighbouring planets.

Yet this triple revolution, one of the most crucial in the history of mankind, is hardly one to look back on with pride. Submarines, aeroplanes and spacecraft all owe their amazingly rapid development over the past eight decades primarily to their uses as weapons of war. Because of this, they are not merely objects of gratification and wonder. They have become objects of dread, and none more so than the submarine—the unseen menace, the master weapon of war beneath the sea.

This book is badly needed, and is unashamedly partisan. It is aimed at the reading public of the Free World, which twice in this century has been brought to the brink of starvation and defeat by submarine warfare—yet which seems quite incapable of understanding that the menace is still there, and in even greater strength than in the two world wars.

Contrary to popular belief, the most dangerous facility of the modern submarine is NOT —solely—its ability to wipe out whole cities with ballistic nuclear missiles. The *conventional* submarine, in its commerce-destroying role, is still the only weapon capable of inflicting economic collapse and starvation on populations dependent on seaborne imports—without any

need for the risk and waste of nuclear bombardment.

Now, obsessed with the nuclear arms race and pursuit of illusory nuclear arms limitation treaties, the Western alliance has allowed itself to become perilously outstripped in conventional weaponry—particularly in the field of anti-submarine defence. It will very soon be possible for the Soviet Union to 'call' the nuclear bluff of the West by launching an all-out offensive on land and sea *without* using nuclear weapons. Unless the West rapidly regains parity in conventional weapons it will have little or no chance of surviving such an onslaught, and certainly not at sea. Over the past twenty years the Soviet Navy has been built up into the second biggest assemblage of conventional sea power in the world, with a submarine fleet dwarfing the numbers of U-boats which brought Germany so close to victory in the two world wars.

*Undersea War*, therefore, is the story of a deadly menace past and present: a menace which, to be fought and defeated, first requires recognition and understanding. It is the earnest hope of the author that this book will contribute to the better understanding of military reality, without which freedom in the world cannot hope to survive.

Previous page: The SS *City of Glasgow*, her back broken by a German torpedo, sinks in the Eastern Atlantic in the last months of the 1st World War.
Left: Launch of USS *Narwhal*, the US Navy's test bed for the new and quieter S&G natural circulation nuclear reactor —September 1967.
Below: The Royal Navy's Valiant-class fleet submarine HMS *Churchill* is followed to sea by the Resolution-class ballistic missile submarine HMS *Renown* in the early 1970s.

# 1. BIRTH OF A WEAPON

Previous pages: The shape
of things to come—
*Nordenfeldt I*, the first
submarine to be fitted with
a bow torpedo tube, under
construction in Sweden in
1882.

Like the aeroplane, the submarine is an artificial aid for overcoming natural laws. An aeroplane's wings create lift to counter its natural tendency to obey gravity; a submarine's ballast tanks enable the ship to counter its natural tendency to float. The aeroplane and the submarine were close contemporaries and by 1900 both were approaching the working-prototype stage. In the case of the submarine, however, one of the vital principles needed to design a boat capable of submerging and re-surfacing at will had been correctly stated over three centuries earlier.

The first clear-cut outline for a submersible warship was drafted in 1578 by an Englishman, William Bourne. He was a gunner attracted by the idea of a warship which could submerge to escape the effects of enemy cannon fire. Bourne wrote an extraordinarily confident book called *The Treasure for Travellers*, proposing a water-tight hull fitted on each side with a flooding chamber like a giant leather concertina, open to the sea;

'and in the inside to have Skrewes to winde it in and also out again; and for to have it sinke, they must wind it in to make the thing lesse, and then it sinketh unto the bottom; and to have it swimme, then to winde the sides out again, to make the thing bigger, and then it will swim, according unto the body of the thing in the water.'

Riddled with practical objections, Bourne's idea was purely abstract and never got further than its outline on paper, but the notion of ballast tanks which must be filled to submerge and evacuated to surface was absolutely right. It was ignored by the Dutchman Cornelis Drebbel, fifty years after Bourne, who made similarly grandiose claims for his oar-powered submersible boats. Two of these took shape in 1620—completely enclosed and sheathed in grease-soaked leather, powered by six oars a side, with each oar passing through a watertight leather sleeve. Each Drebbel submersible was ballasted with heavy weights until it was just awash, the efforts of the oarsmen then driving the boat below the surface. Here was another

Right: Cornelis Drebbel, whose oared submersible of 1520 had two-thirds of the hull weighed below the water-line by ballast. The 'nose-down' slant of the upper carapace assisted the labouring oarsmen to drive the boat beneath the surface. Though with distinct overtones of alchemy, Drebbel was the first on record to tackle the problem of air replenishment.

principle adopted by 'real' submarines when their time finally came: that a submarine, proceeding under its own power and wishing to dive, first reduces its buoyancy to the minimum and then uses its own momentum to drive itself under the surface.

Though Drebbel's most obvious problem was the near-impossibility of making his boats fully watertight, the aspect of his formula which attracted most attention was that of air replenishment. He claimed to have discovered a mystic ingredient for renovating the air inside his leather-clad galleys, thus sparing the crews from suffocation. This claim greatly interested the English natural philosopher Robert Boyle (1627–91), who conducted his own research into the matter and recorded

'So that (for ought I could gather) besides the Mechanicall contrivance of his vessel [Drebbel] had a chymicall liquor, which he accounted the chiefe Secret of his submarine Navigation. For when from time to time he perceiv'd, that the finer and purer part of the Air was consum'd, or over clogg'd by the respiration, and steames of those that went in his ship, he would, by unstopping a vessell full of this liquor, speedily restore to the troubled Air such a proportion of vitall parts, as would make it againe, for a good while, fit for Respiration.'

All this, of course, was well over a century before Lavoisier revealed the basic composition of air, with the conflicting influences of oxygen and carbon dioxide ($CO_2$). Air replenishment in submarines remained a problem unsolved until after World War II, with regular tests on the $CO_2$ content of the ship's air and special apparatus to 'scrub' the $CO_2$ out of the air. Until then all submariners had to endure the fetid atmosphere created by excess $CO_2$, and regular surfacing to ventilate the ship remained essential. But the fact that Drebbel claimed to have perfected a primitive '$CO_2$ scrubber' as early as 1620 is another example of the flashes of prescience shown by early submarine pioneers, long before science and technology had placed sufficient knowledge at their disposal.

An enterprising Frenchman named de Son was one of the first inventors on record to design a semi-submersible *warship*. During the first Anglo-Dutch War (1652–54) de Son persuaded the Dutch to build the prototype of a truly wonderful raider—apparently just what the Dutch were looking for to protect the fleets of

PERFECTE AFBEELDINGE VAN 'T WONDERLYCKE SCHIP GEMAAKT TOT ROTTERDAM 1653

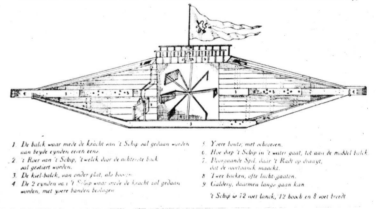

their East India Company and hurt those of the English. 'He doth undertake in one day to destroy a honderd ships, can goe from Rotterdam to London and back againe in one day, and in six weeks to goe to the East Indiens, and to run as swift as a bird can flye, no fire, no storme, no bullets, can hinder her, unlesse it please God.' De Son's boat was duly built at Rotterdam in 1653, but none of the nonsensical claims which he made for her were ever put to the test. The massive timbers of the framework proved too much for the clockwork paddlewheel chosen to power the boat, and she refused to move an inch.

De Son's boat certainly belongs to the lunatic fringe of projects which have helped to foster the image of the crackpot inventor down the ages, but it is not without interest. It had no conventional bow or stern: each end terminated in an iron-shod ram for sinking ships below the waterline. Steered by side rudders and conned from an upper gallery, the boat was designed to lie as low in the water as possible, under the

De Son's 'wonderful ship' under construction at Rotterdam in 1653. The inventor's claims for the boat envisaged a global role against the enemies of the Dutch seaborne empire. But de Son's clockwork paddlewheel proved less than adequate as a powerplant for such a massive structure.

Opposite: Starboard exterior, plan view and cutaway of Bushnell's *Turtle* (1776). The ballast tanks can be seen beneath the operator's feet ('O'), together with the pumps ('P' and 'Q') for flooding and evacuating the tanks. To the left of the vertical screw can be seen the gimlet ('R') for piercing the target's bottom planking; this is connected to the detachable explosive charge ('S').

broadside line of fire of conventional sail warships. Its angular, sloped streamlining to deflect shot and present a deliberately awkward target, was centuries ahead of its time. Indeed, one of the most notable features of de Son's boat is the startling resemblance of its silhouette to the pioneer ironclads *Merrimac* and *Monitor* in the American Civil War, 200 years later. De Son had designed a low-silhouette boat intended to launch deadly attacks on the surface, using both ends of its longitudinal axis when circumstances permitted—rudiments of attack which German U-boats, armed with bow and stern torpedo tubes, were to perfect when penetrating Allied convoys between 1940 and 1943.

The potentialities of submersible vessels continued to attract attention during the increasing upsurge of scientific enquiry in the Middle and late 17th century. In 1648 an Oxford don, Dr John Wilkins of Wadham College (a future founder-member of the Royal Society) published a short treatise on the subject which was amazingly farsighted. Accepting that the day of the submarine had yet to dawn, he described what it could be like in glowing terms. To Wilkins the role of the submarine in war, striking down orthodox surface warships from beneath the waves, was only a disagreeable sideshoot, almost a perversion. He preferred to look forward to the day when submarine craft would carry merchandise in safety from storm and tempest, salvage cargo from wrecked ships, carry out underwater fishing and even, he suggested, ply between manned undersea colonies. It would be wrong to hail Wilkins as the Jacques-Yves Cousteau of the 17th century; Wilkins was one of the gifted scientific amateurs of the age, overwhelmed by the new urge to query all past assumptions and constantly darting from one intriguing scientific topic to the next. During that unique century when men were probing for the natural laws of the Universe itself—the century of Kepler and Galileo, Newton and Leibnitz—the problems surrounding underwater navigation often seemed petty indeed.

For all that, men kept trying. In 1679 an Italian priest, Father Borelli, came up with a design which blended Bourne's flexible ballast chambers with Drebbel's enclosed, oar-propelled hull. For increasing and reducing buoyancy as required, Borelli suggested a cluster of water-skins (each one open to the sea via a vent) which could be individually collapsed and tied off, later to be re-inflated, by the crew. Broad-bladed oars would propel the

craft both on the surface and when submerged. When the Borelli formula was finally tried out in 1747, by the Englishman Symons on the River Thames, it was found that the space taken up by the leather ballast chambers left no room for oarsmen. Symons did, however, prove that the theory of flooding and evacuating ballast chambers was the right way of getting a sealed hull to decrease or increase its buoyancy.

Such were the leading experiments, crude though they were, made in the 17th century with submersible or semi-submersible craft. From the outset no one doubted that a submarine, stealthily approaching beneath the surface, would have a wonderful advantage in attacking orthodox enemy fleets. But assuming that such a craft could be built, how could the actual attack be carried out? As we have seen, de Son had favoured the classic ploy of ramming. But the first method actually used in a submarine attack, that of blasting the victim with a detachable explosive charge, can also be traced back to the 17th century.

In the year 1650, blockaded in the Tagus by an English Parliamentarian fleet under Admiral Robert Blake, Prince Rupert of the Rhine devised a primitive torpedo to drive off his enemies. This had to be conveyed to the victim in a small surface craft and detonated by remote control when in position. Rupert's torpedo (perhaps 'portable mine' would be a better description) was splendidly described as 'a bomb ball in a double-headed barrel with a lock in the bowels to give fire to a quick match'. It was an ignominious failure because Blake's men saw it coming—but it was nevertheless the first attempt to destroy an enemy ship with a blasting charge placed on or just below the waterline, and deserves remembrance on that score.

Like Prince Rupert's 'bomb ball', the next attempt at a submersible ship sought to break the blockade of an otherwise unbeatable conventional surface fleet. The result was unprecedented: not only a workable submarine craft, but one able to carry out an attack which came hearteningly close to success. It happened in 1776, the first year of outright hostilities between Britain and her American colonies. Among the 'Patriots', as the American rebels called themselves, few were more patriotic than David Bushnell, who graduated from Yale University in 1775. Bushnell realised that the biggest weakness of the Patriots in their struggle against Britain was the ability of the Royal Navy to strike where it chose along the American

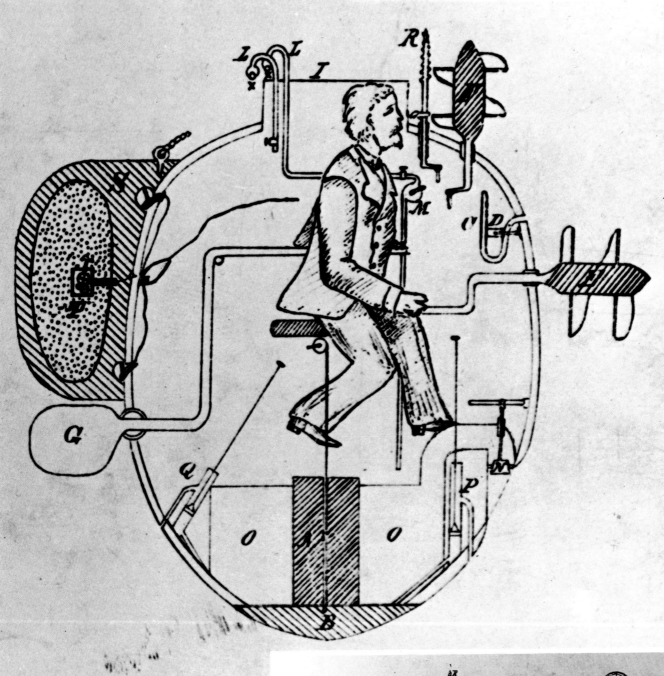

coastline, and he resolved to produce a submarine vessel capable of counterattacking British warships on equal terms.

The result was the famous *Turtle*, the first midget submarine. *Turtle* was a floating egg, kept upright in the water by a lead keel. The solitary crewman had no lack of things to push, pull and twirl in order to manoeuvre the boat and maintain its vertical trim. A single brass hand-pump forced seawater into the tank beneath his feet; another hand-pump forced the water out again when the time came to surface. A forward-pointing hand-turned screw provided horizontal propulsion; a vertical screw

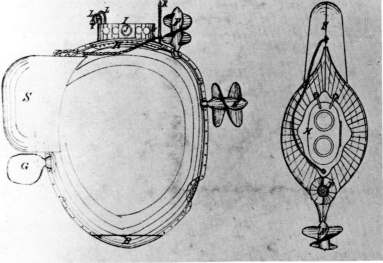

enabled *Turtle* to be nudged up and down without disturbing the trim in the buoyancy tank. Lateral control was provided by a small rudder and tiller. A small porthole at the operator's eye level helped him see where he was going as *Turtle* struggled through the water with only the operator's head, encased in the upper hatch mounting, showing above the surface.

That Bushnell was able to become the first man to manoeuvre, dive and surface at will in this craft was achievement enough, but *Turtle* was designed as an offensive weapon. The idea was to get right under the hull of the target after an unobtrusive approach under cover of darkness. The operator would then try to force a long gimlet, mounted through *Turtle's* upper shell, up into the victim's bottom planking. This gimlet was detachable and was connected to a sealed explosive charge, also detachable. Once driven securely home, the gimlet would be detached and the charge with it, the latter being fired by a long lanyard paid out from the now-retreating *Turtle*.

The man who volunteered to take *Turtle* into action in August 1776 was Sergeant Ezra Lee of the Patriot Army; the enemy force attacked was the fleet of Admiral Howe blockading New York in the late summer of 1776; and the ship singled out as *Turtle's* victim was no less than Howe's flagship, HMS *Eagle*, a 64-gun ship anchored in the lower Hudson River. *Turtle* was towed upstream of *Eagle* before being turned loose to drift down on her prey. Lee had no trouble during his approach and fetched up triumphantly under *Eagle's* stern. Then his troubles began. He had to fight with a powerful tidal current to keep *Turtle* in position, heavy work at the screws alternating with frantic twists at the gimlet. But nobody had told Bushnell of the new British policy of protecting ships' bottoms from the ravages of the teredo

*Turtle* goes to war: the attack on HMS *Eagle* in August 1776.

worm with copper sheeting, and despite Lee's efforts *Turtle*'s gimlet refused to bite. Lee most gallantly kept trying until his air supply began to run out, finally accepting defeat as daylight approached. As he wrestled *Turtle* clear of the *Eagle* he was spotted and pursued by boats' crews but had the satisfaction of slipping the explosive charge and detonating it in the faces of the British, which covered his escape.

Even if Lee's attack had met with the success it so richly deserved and had blown up one of Britain's leading admirals in his flagship, nothing could have prevented the British from taking New York, which they did in September 1776. They were in overwhelming strength and *Turtle*'s foray was an insignificant, if supremely gallant gesture. When all is said and done it was a failure and the Americans can hardly be blamed for not building a fleet of *Turtle*s as the War of Independence ground ahead. Loss of supremacy at sea eventually made it certain that the British would lose the war, but this was

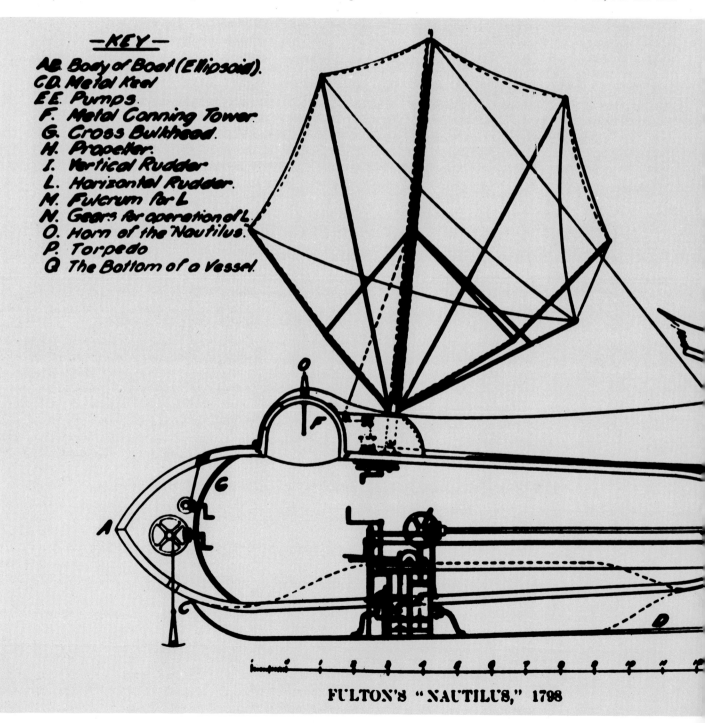

—KEY—

AB. Body of Boat (Ellipsoid).
CD. Metal Keel
EE. Pumps.
F. Metal Conning Tower.
G. Cross Bulkhead.
H. Propeller.
I. Vertical Rudder.
L. Horizontal Rudder.
M. Fulcrum for L
N. Gears for operation of L.
O. Horn of the Nautilus.
P. Torpedo
Q. The Bottom of a Vessel.

FULTON'S "NAUTILUS," 1798

Left: Robert Fulton was a submarine inventor decades ahead of his time.
Opposite: The plans of Fulton's *Nautilus*.

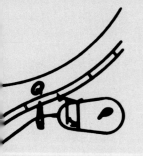

not brought about by American sea power. It was the work of America's most potent ally, the Navy of Bourbon France. *Turtle* did not survive the war, being sunk by the British while being ferried across the river. When the war ended in 1782, Bushnell abandoned his work on submarines, changed his name and became a doctor, dying in 1824. But he had produced the first submarine able to dive, surface, stalk its prey and carry out an attack.

Such a consolation was denied the next man to build a submarine: another American, Robert Fulton, born in 1765. He was a strange character, a supremely gifted all-rounder who decided to devote himself to engineering after early life first as an apprentice jeweller, then as a professional painter. In 1797, having failed to interest English canal companies in his idea for replacing lock gates by hauling boats up inclined planes, he crossed to Paris. There he spent the next four years trying to persuade the French Navy to build a fleet of submarines with which to destroy the victorious fleets of Britain. At last, after obtaining a grant of 10,000 francs from Napoleon in 1801, Fulton designed and built the *Nautilus*.

She was slug-shaped, 21 feet long and seven feet in diameter. Like *Turtle*, *Nautilus* submerged by means of internal ballast tanks. *Nautilus* was a greatly superior design, not least because she was big enough to take a crew of two or even three men. This left the commander, who stood in the bows with his head in an observation dome, free to give his undivided attention to directing the boat. *Nautilus* was the first submarine to adopt one form of propulsion for the surface and an alternative system for proceeding when submerged. She used a collapsible mast and sail when on the surface and a hand-cranked screw when submerged. The attack procedure was the same as Bushnell's: a detachable gimlet and explosive charge. *Nautilus*, however, featured a small bow anchor to hold her in position beneath the victim's hull while the charge was attached.

The first diving trials, carried out in the Seine, were completely successful and *Nautilus* was taken to Brest for trials in the open sea. Fulton carried out a perfect submerged attack against an old schooner moored in the harbour, blowing her open and sinking her. But the aftermath of this triumph was completely unexpected. Far from exulting at this new master-weapon placed at their disposal, the French Ministry of Marine turned it down flat. The reason was that it was a weapon too dangerous to use—that if used, any enemy could turn it against the original user with even more deadly effect. The French rejected Fulton and his *Nautilus* and so did the British, when the latter were given a chance to evaluate it by the Peace of Amiens (March 1802–May 1803). When William Pitt returned to office as Prime Minister in the following year he favoured the adoption of the Fulton submarine, but the veteran Admiral of the Fleet, Earl St Vincent, set his face against it. 'Pitt was the greatest fool that ever existed', growled St Vincent, 'to encourage a mode of warfare which those who commanded the seas did not want and which, if successful, would at once deprive them of it.'

This rejection of Fulton and his submarine by the two leading 'superpowers' of the age was a unique moment in the history of modern warfare. Both sides turned down the new weapon not because it was impractical or absurd, but because it was only too efficient! After meeting with yet a third rejection in his native United States, Fulton turned from submarines to steamboat design. He is still remembered for having introduced the first steamboat to carry a regular passenger service. This was the *Clermont* (1807) which plied between New York and Albany on the Hudson River—the waters where Bushnell's *Turtle* had made her debut nearly 40 years before.

Thirty-five years after Fulton died, in 1815, another submarine was being designed across the Atlantic, in Germany: the *Seetaucher* or 'Sea Diver' (also known by the French name, *Plongeur-Marin*). *Seetaucher* was the brainchild

Bauer's *Le Diable-Marin* on the bottom of Kronstadt harbour on Tsar Alexander II's coronation day (1856). The four-piece band embarked for the occasion stands to the right of the two-man treadmill used to drive the screw.

of a Bavarian non-commissioned officer, Wilhelm Bauer. She was designed and built in a hurry for exactly the same reason as Bushnell's *Turtle*: to challenge an enemy blockade. The blockade in question was being imposed on Kiel by the Danish Navy during the war between Denmark and Prussia over the duchies of Schleswig and Holstein (1849–50). *Seetaucher* was completed too late for the war, and when she was tested at Kiel in February 1851 the disastrous flaws in her design became only too apparent.

Unlike *Turtle* and *Nautilus* with their rounded cross-sections, *Seetaucher* was a narrow, slab-sided rectangle of iron plating. She contained some of the salient features of *Nautilus* (internal ballast tanks, crew of three and a hand-cranked screw) but Bauer had introduced a novel idea: a weight sliding fore and aft to alter the horizontal trim of the boat. When Bauer and his two crewmen attempted their first dive in *Seetaucher*, the boat's narrow lines caused her bow to drop too swiftly; the weight slid violently forward, all control was lost and she plunged to the bottom in 60 feet of water. As she went down the sudden increase in water pressure stove in her flat side plating and water flooded in. Bauer, however, trapped in an air pocket with his crew, kept his head. He allowed more water to flood in until

the air pressure within the wreck equalled the water pressure outside, then cracked open the hatch and struck out for the surface with his men, helped upwards by the escaping bubble of air from the boat. All three reached the surface in safety—the first submarine escapers to use the principle of equalised pressures still used in escape drill today.

Undeterred by this near-disaster and a host of other setbacks over the next five years, Bauer kept revising his designs until, in 1855, he came up with the cylindrical *Le Diable-Marin*—the 'Sea Devil'. She was sponsored by the Imperial Russian Navy as a hopeful means of challenging the tight Franco-British blockade of the Russian Baltic coast during the Crimean War (1854–56). *Le Diable-Marin* was the biggest submarine which had ever been built: 52 feet long, 12 feet in diameter, and powered by a central two-man treadmill. She was not completed in time to see action in the Crimean War but created a sensation at the coronation of Tsar Alexander II. On 6 September 1856, at Kronstadt, Bauer embarked a quartet of musicians who played patriotic tunes from the bottom of the harbour throughout the new Tsar's coronation day. This timely piece of showmanship, directly comparable to the first submarine voyage to the North Pole in the 1950s (if of somewhat less scientific value) did much to establish the submarine as something more than an outlandish flirtation with fantasy. *Le Diable-Marin* subsequently became the first submarine to make over 100 successful dives, but was lost on the 135th.

Within ten years of Bauer's propaganda exercise at Kronstadt, the submarine had made the transition into reality by proving its worth as a weapon of war. Once again the stimulus was that of a nation threatened with defeat by a hostile naval blockade—the hard-pressed Southern Confederacy in the American Civil War (1861–65). In March 1862 the Confederate Navy made history when its experimental ironclad *Merrimac* sank two Northern warships off Norfolk, Virginia, and went on to fight an epic if inconclusive duel with the Northern ironclad *Monitor*. And in the following year the Confederates did it again, with the first of two resounding attacks on Northern ironclads by semi-submersible craft known as 'Davids'.

The 'Davids' were basically manned torpedoes for smashing into the sides of their victims. The original *David* could not submerge as it was steam-powered, with its crew of four given the precarious safety of a one-man hatch just above the waterline. She carried a 60-pound explosive charge at the end of a long spar extended from the bow. On the night of 5 October 1863 Lieutenant W T Gassell and three volunteers sortied from Charleston to attack the massive ironclad NSS *New Ironsides*, which had already

Another naval 'first' for the Confederate Navy in the American Civil War: *David*'s spar torpedo explodes against the armour of USS *New Ironsides* off Charleston (5 October 1863).

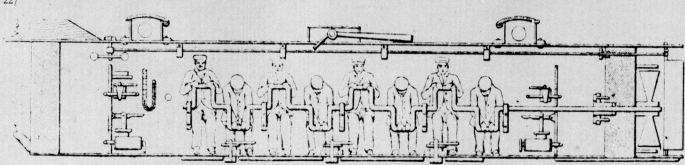

*Fig 3*

Water line when ballasted to Sink

water line light

Right: The Confederate 'David' *Hunley* (1864) was the first submersible to sink an enemy warship. To offset the combined weight of the human 'pistons' (above), all of whom crouched on the starboard side of the crankshaft (left), she needed all the stability which her primitive hydroplanes could provide.
Below: A steam-powered 'David' aground at Charleston at the end of the Civil War.

survived over 250 heavy-calibre hits from the Confederate guns in Charleston's Fort Sumter. Though spotted during her final approach, *David* struck home fair and square on the waterline of *New Ironsides*. A huge explosion swamped *David* and Gassell abandoned ship, but *David* stayed afloat, being salvaged and brought back to Charleston by her pilot and fireman.

During the attack, Acting Ensign C W Howard, USN, became the first man to be killed in a submarine attack. He had hailed the strange craft as it closed *New Ironsides*, only to fall mortally wounded to the blast of a shotgun fired from *David*'s hatch. *New Ironsides* suffered nothing worse than strained iron plates and a bad leak, but the experiment encouraged the Southerners to build more 'Davids'. The next to attack (also at Charleston) was the *H L Hunley*. This 'David' was powered by an eight-man crankshaft and featured an important innovation to submarine design: horizontal adjustable planes to control the boat's fore-and-aft trim. On the night of 17 February 1864 the *Hunley*'s spar torpedo blew an enormous hole in the (wooden) USS *Housatonic*. The Northern ship sank, but unfortunately the blast and turbulence of the explosion swamped and sank the *Hunley* with her entire crew.

At the end of the American Civil War in 1865 the evolution of the submarine had reached a critical stage. Two daunting obstacles would somehow have to be overcome if the submarine were not to remain a lumbering toy, able to do no more than attack anchored targets under cover of darkness.

The first of these obstacles was power. As improvements in steam propulsion continued, targets for submarine attacks were bound to become faster, more agile, and virtually impossible for submarines to catch. Muscle power for submarines was clearly obsolete; apart from its other limitations it used up too much air in the boat. But putting a steam engine in a submarine only tied the craft to the surface. Somehow a new power system had to be devised which would give submarines a decent turn of speed on the surface, without being deprived of the ability to dive and continue under power when submerged.

The second obstacle was the immense danger posed by the spar torpedo, as the 'Davids' had found to their cost. For a sea power weak in conventional warships, the submarine's biggest virtue was the chance it offered of counterattacking more powerful fleets on equal terms. But if every submarine attack meant the total loss of the submarine, the strategic economy of the craft vanished. Suicide attacks would not only make submarines a prohibitive and wasteful investment, but make it virtually impossible to find the men to crew them. Some form of long-range weapon was needed, one which

could be fired—preferably when submerged—without risking the total loss of the submarine.

The second problem was the first to be overcome, with the appearance of the first Luppis-Whitehead 'locomotive torpedo' in the late 1860s. This was a self-propelled explosive charge, capable when launched of running in a straight line to the target. Early torpedoes contained as many 'bugs' as early submarines; they, too, needed an efficient power plant (compressed air) and some contrivance (the gyroscope) to keep them running straight and level. But by the middle 1880s it was clear that a Whitehead torpedo fired from a tube, which could be done either on the surface or just below, was going to be the submarine's natural weapon.

In the three decades after the American Civil War international interest in submarines accelerated, with more and more pooling, borrowing and copying of ideas. In 1879, for instance, the English clergyman G W Garrett designed and built the *Resurgam* ('I will rise again'). Her steam engine operated normally on the surface but stored steam in pressure cylinders for driving the boat when submerged. Garrett's system was taken up by the Swedish gunsmith Nordenfeldt, whose *Nordenfeldt I* (1882) was the first

Below and opposite, below: Typical of the spindle-shaped, sharp-ended designs after the American Civil War was Garrett's *Resurgam*. Her engine stored steam in pressure tanks for driving the boat when submerged. Inset shows cross-section of hull (still carvel-built from timber baulks) in front of the engine-room.

submarine to be fitted with a torpedo tube. The French designers Goubet and Dupuy de Lôme, and the Spaniard Don Isaac Peral, experimented with electric-powered submarines in the 1880s, power being supplied by banks of batteries which needed frequent recharging. In the USA the most influential designer of them all, John P Holland, produced a series of experimental boats throughout the 1880s which finally bore fruit in the *Holland VII* (1895) and *Holland VIII* (1900). The latter served as the prototype for every submarine adopted by the world's navies

down to 1914. She had a petroleum engine for surface propulsion, an electric engine for running submerged, a torpedo tube and a deck gun. The only major change before 1914 was the general adoption of the diesel engine in preference to the petrol engine with its volatile fuel. The diesel/electric power combination for submarines is still in widespread use today and until the advent of nuclear power in the 1950s, which allowed the wheel to come full circle and steam propulsion to be used both on the surface and below, it was the safest and most efficient.

*Nordenfeldt I* as completed showing the tiny flank motors for submerged propulsion.

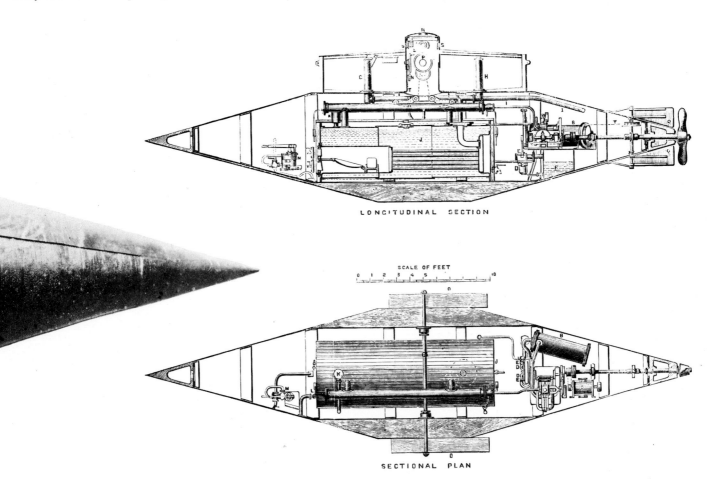

LONGITUDINAL SECTION

SCALE OF FEET

SECTIONAL PLAN

Below: American break-through, *Holland*, commissioned into the US Navy in 1900. Right: Cadets at the US Naval Academy being introduced to a *Holland*-type submarine in 1902.

The young Imperial German Navy began with two Nordenfeldt-type boats in 1890 and in 1902 produced its ultra-secret, all-electric *Howalt* with its single bow torpedo. Valuable experience was gained with her and with three oil/electric submarines (*Karp*, *Karas* and *Kambala*) built for the Russian Navy by Krupp's Germania Yard. Finally, in 1906, the German Navy ordered its first *unterseeboot*: *U-1*, powered by kerosene/electric motors. With all the reluctance which Earl St Vincent had shown towards Fulton's *Nautilus* a century before, Britain came late into the field; but in 1901 the British also began to build up a submarine fleet with the purchase of five *Holland* boats from the USA.

By the summer of 1914 not one of the world's leading naval powers lacked some form of submarine force. The role of the new weapon had yet to be defined and its immense potential for destruction caused widespread misgiving. One English admiral, Sir Arthur Wilson, had suggested as early as 1902 that the crews of

Above: Britain's *Holland*-type 'Submarine No 3' cruises symbolically past Nelson's *Victory*.

captured submarines in war should be hanged as pirates. At the same time he described submarines as 'underhand, unfair and damned un-English'. But two years later Admiral Sir John Fisher was writing that 'I don't think it is even *faintly* realised—*the immense impending revolution which the submarines will effect as offensive weapons of war*'. Within ten years that revolution had already been recognised, before the first shot of World War I had even been fired. The mighty British Grand Fleet of Dreadnought battleships and battle-cruisers, easily the world's strongest, was under orders to hold back at its remote base at Scapa Flow in the Orkneys, safely out of reach of German submarines. In less than a century and a half the comical silhouette of Bushnell's *Turtle* had grown and elongated into the sinister shadow of the U-boat.

# 2. 1914-1939

30 /

Previous pages: The 'ace of aces' in action—Arnauld de la Perière's *U-35* firing at her latest victim. De la Perière scorned the use of the costly torpedo, preferring to add to his staggering totals of tonnage sunk by means of gunfire on the surface. With this tactic he became the most successful submariner of all time, sinking 189 ships totalling 446,708 tons between November 1915 and March 1918.

When World War I began in August 1914 the role of the submarine was obscured by a cloud of doubts, hopes and fears about what submarines *could* do and above all, what they *should* do. This applied to both of the two leading naval antagonists, Britain and Germany. For the previous ten years they had been obsessed with the race to build the strongest conventional fleet of battleships, and the British and Imperial German Navies had built submarines largely because everyone else had them. The British had taken to the submarine with all the more reluctance, because the submarine was seen as a sneaky underhand weapon to use against any honest surface fleet. As for the suggestion that enemy submarines might be used against merchant shipping, this would be such a barbaric violation of the rules of 'civilised' war that it was generally dismissed as unthinkable.

These rules, tentatively defined by the Hague Peace Conferences of 1899 and 1907, had laid it down that a warship wishing to sink an enemy merchant ship must first stop its victim, give clear warning of its intention, and afterwards provide for the safety of the castaway crew. Neutrals could be stopped and searched, and if found to be carrying war materials for a hostile power could be escorted to port and interned. But a few far-sighted men, headed in Britain by Admiral Lord Fisher, had by 1914 realised with growing apprehension that the submarine was a weapon to which such rules could not apply. The submarine, Fisher pointed out in a memorandum of January 1914, 'cannot capture the merchant ship; she has no spare hands to put a prize crew on board; little or nothing would be gained by disabling her engines or propeller; she cannot convey her into harbour; and, in fact, it is impossible for the submarine to deal with commerce in the light and provisions of accepted international law.' And he went on: 'There is nothing else the submarine can do except sink her capture ... this submarine menace is a terrible one for British commerce and Great Britain alike, for no means can be suggested at present of meeting it except by reprisals.'

Prophetic words indeed, but they were regarded as fantastic by the British government and Admiralty alike and subsequently ignored. So far from deducing that submarines would, by reason of their very limitations, have no option but to sink their prey, the Admiralty had declared in a memorandum of December 1912 that the submarine had the smallest value of any

vessel for attacks on trade. 'Therefore she will not affect the direct action in attack, which must be made by cruisers and other surface travelling vessels.'

This wishful thinking, that submarine attacks on merchant shipping would be considered *tabu*, was in total contrast to the conviction that warships were predestined targets for submarine attack. One of the commonest features on battleships, battle-cruisers and heavy cruisers down to 1914 was the distinctive diagonal barring of ships' sides with long booms, which could be swung out at right-angles to protect the ship with anti-torpedo nets when she lay at anchor. By 1914 the submarine was accepted, along with surface torpedo-boats and mines, as one of the three most insidious menaces to heavy surface warships. And the British, hag-ridden by the fear of having their numerical superiority in capital ships whittled away by German torpedoes and mines, were taking the submarine threat to their naval superiority very seriously indeed.

As far as the all-important North Sea theatre was concerned, British naval strategy in 1914 was the offspring of a weird marriage of confidence and fear. The confidence was that (for some reason best known to the German Admiralty) the outnumbered German High Seas Fleet would decide to come out and fight. The fear was that cumulative British losses from German mines and torpedoes would enable the High Seas Fleet eventually to fight a battle on even terms. Thus nothing would be gained by a close blockade of German ports— the British *wanted* the Germans to come out and fight. On the other hand it would be clearly suicidal for the British to court piecemeal destruction by the mine-and-torpedo menace. By 1912, therefore, unknown to the German Admiralty, the British had already decided against a close blockade of German ports in the event of war. Instead the massed battle squadrons of the British Grand Fleet would be held as far north as possible in Scottish waters, close enough to pounce on any sortie into the North Sea by the High Seas Fleet, but at extreme range from German submarine and torpedo attack. The huge natural anchorage of Scapa Flow in the Orkneys was finally chosen as the Grand Fleet's war base.

The Germans had no intention of throwing themselves into a sea war; they were gambling on a knockout victory on land, at the expense of the French and German Armies. German naval strategy was strictly opportunist. Warships already at sea were to make as big a nuisance of themselves on the high seas as possible, hopefully drawing off large numbers of British warships in pursuit. Lone British warships and isolated squadrons were to be lured to their doom in German coastal waters, either amid the dense minefields screening the German bases or under the guns of the High Seas Fleet in superior strength. But when the Grand Fleet stayed where it was in Scapa Flow, the embryo and untried U-boat force was sent out to attempt to carry the war into British waters.

At the outbreak of the war the German Navy only had 20 U-boats fit for service, and four of these (*U-1*, *U-2*, *U-3* and *U-4*) were suitable only for training. *U-5* to *U-18*, inclusive, were all powered by Körting heavy-oil engines which emitted sparks and dense clouds of white smoke when running on the surface; only three of the 18 bigger diesel-engined boats ordered in 1912–13 had been completed by August 1914, and the completion of the other 15 dragged on until October 1915. But on 6 August 1914, with the war barely 48 hours old, *Korvettenkapitän* Hermann Bauer led the first U-boat sortie into the North Sea. With ten U-boats (all of them heavy-oil boats) he planned to cruise to the Grand Fleet's front doorstep: a line from the Shetlands to Bergen in Norway.

This operation, the first joint war cruise by a flotilla of submarines, met with a funereal lack of success. Engine failure forced *U-9* to head back to base on 8 August. On the same day a British battle squadron was sighted off Fair Isle, midway between the Orkneys and Shetlands; *U-13* and *U-15* went in to attack, but the only torpedo fired missed the Dreadnought battleship *Monarch* and alerted the British force. Then *U-15*, separated from the rest of the flotilla, was surprised on the surface at dawn on the 9th by the light cruiser *Birmingham*. The British warship opened fire at once and increased speed to ram. As *Birmingham* came in for the kill her men heard hammering noises coming from inside *U-15*'s hull, suggesting that the U-boat had been crippled by main engine failure which her crew was trying to repair to the last. This was never confirmed because *Birmingham's* stem sliced *U-15* completely in two, the two halves of the U-boat going down with her entire complement of 29. And when, on the 12th, Bauer and the surviving U-boats returned to Heligoland, they heard that a second of their number had been lost. This was *U-13*, which had strayed into a German minefield and been sunk

German World War I painting of the scene in a U-boat's control room.

quickly and quietly on 9 August.

A second U-boat sweep had been sent out on 8 August, while Bauer and his men were still at sea. This was prompted by extraordinarily inaccurate German intelligence, which had surmised that the British Expeditionary Force was already at sea and heading for a landfall in Belgium. (In fact the BEF did not sail until a week later, and when it did it disembarked in France.) Four of the new diesel-engined U-boats sailed to intercept the non-existent British transports. The diesel boats had been rushed into service; 'teething troubles' were naturally rife, and three of them turned back with mechanical defects. Only *Kapitänleutnant* Otto Hersing in *U-21* reached the patrol area, to return empty-handed.

These first cruises, however, were of immense value. They gave German submariners their first vital operational experience, and located mechanical and design weaknesses which could be tackled and either overcome or omitted from new boats. Apart from this the first U-boat sorties, so far to the north, not only confirmed the 'submarine neurosis' of the British Grand Fleet but raised it to ever higher levels. False economy in the last two years of peace had left Scapa Flow—unlike the German North Sea bases—without any artificial defences capable of keeping out enemy submarines. There were no booms, no lines of blockships, no shore searchlights, no belts of mines sealing the channels between the islands of Orkney ringing the Flow. Nor had any weapons been developed capable of attacking a submerged submarine. 'Anti-submarine picket-boats' nervously patrolled the Flow, preposterously armed with large bags and hammers: the bag was for

/

Admiral Sir John Jellicoe, according to Churchill, was 'the only man who could have lost the war in an afternoon'. Jellicoe commanded the world's mightiest battle fleet — and found his tactical movements paralysed by fears of the German submarine menace.

ramming over a conveniently presented periscope, the hammer for smashing the periscope lens.

As a result any freak ripple, any lone seal putting its head up was likely to be reported as a periscope, sending the world's mightiest battle fleet stampeding out to sea and safety. It happened for the first time on 1 September 1914 and Admiral Sir John Jellicoe kept the Grand Fleet at sea for four days before he deemed it safe to return. Even then he only sent the 3rd Battle Squadron back to Scapa, taking the bulk of the Fleet to Loch Ewe on the west coast of Scotland. While the panic was at its height, Otto Hersing came probing into the Firth of Forth in *U-21*. He was spotted and chased out to sea, but on the afternoon of the 5th, off St Abb's Head, *U-21* fell in with the British light cruiser *Pathfinder* and her destroyer flotilla. In seas so rough that the British could not at first believe that a torpedo attack had been made, Hersing fired a single torpedo which sent the little cruiser to the bottom with the loss of 259 of her complement of 296. The U-boat arm had claimed its first victim.

The withdrawal of the Grand Fleet to the west coast of Scotland because of the U-boat panic must be counted one of the greatest missed opportunities of World War I. If the German naval Zeppelins had discovered that the Grand Fleet was neither in the North Sea nor in Scapa, there would have been nothing to prevent the full strength of the High Seas Fleet from sweeping into the English Channel, severing the BEF's communications with home on the eve of the Battle of the Marne.

Within three weeks of Hersing's kill off St Abb's Head the U-boat arm struck again—and this time resoundingly. On 22 September 1914 *Kapitänleutnant* Otto Weddigen, in *U-9*, became the only submarine captain in naval history to sink three enemy cruisers in a single hour. The ships in question were the old *Cressy* class cruisers *Aboukir*, *Hogue* and *Cressy* (completed in 1901–02) and on the morning of the 22nd they were parading up and down the southeastern stretch of the North Sea known as the 'Broad Fourteens'. There was no compelling reason for maintaining this exposed beat, perilously close to German waters—other than the damning comment of the Admiralty Chief of Staff that 'We've *always* maintained a squadron on the Broad Fourteens'. But nor was there any compelling reason to order their withdrawal, and the Admiralty neglected to do so. The cruisers were screened

by two destroyer flotillas from Harwich, but these were forced back to base by bad weather on the 17th, leaving the ageing trio on its own; and the cruisers were still patrolling the 'Broad Fourteens' when Weddigen found them on the morning of 22 September.

A stiff wind was kicking up five-foot 'white-caps' on the sea and the British lookouts had failed to spot *U-9*'s periscope when Weddigen fired his first bow torpedo at *Aboukir* at 6.30 am. He fired submerged at a depth of about 12 feet, allowing his torpedo a straight run without being deflected by the wave crests, and scored a direct hit. Captain Drummond of the *Aboukir* believed that he had hit a mine, and made the fatal error of ordering *Hogue* and *Cressy* to close and assist. They stopped and lowered boats, presenting Weddigen with two perfectly positioned, stationary targets. He could not miss, and at 7.30 am *Cressy* followed *Hogue* and *Aboukir* to the bottom. Weddigen had made excellent use of the tumbling seas as camouflage, never showing enough periscope to give the British a solitary clue to their tormentor's whereabouts. The Harwich destroyers had sailed to rejoin the cruisers early the same morning; they finally came pounding up to the scene of the disaster, but not in time to prevent the loss of 1459 officers and men out of 2200. The destroyers tried to intercept Weddigen as he withdrew to a hero's welcome in Germany, but he evaded them with ease.

With the war not seven weeks old, the 'damned unEnglish' weapon had inflicted one of the most humiliating and one-sided defeats in the history of the Royal Navy. '*More men lost than by Lord Nelson in all his battles put together!*' raged Lord Fisher. Weddigen's feat did nothing for the morale of the Grand Fleet. 'I *long* for a submarine defence at Scapa; it would give me such a feeling of confidence. I can't sleep half so well inside as when outside, mainly because I feel we are risking such a mass of valuable ships in a place where, if a submarine did get in, she practically has the British Dreadnought Fleet at her mercy.' Those were not the words of an apprehensive midshipman but of the Grand Fleet C-in-C, Admiral Jellicoe, writing to First Lord Winston Churchill on 30 September. And the U-boat arm continued to give substance to Jellicoe's fears. On 15 October Weddigen and *U-9* struck again, this time at the Northern Patrol of old cruisers enforcing the blockade of Germany between Scotland and Norway. East of Aberdeen, Weddigen stalked three *Edgar* class cruisers which frustrated him for hours

with repeated changes of course and speed—one of the earliest and most efficacious anti-submarine measures adopted by the British. Then, suddenly, *Hawke* dropped her guard and hove-to in order to pick up mail from her consort *Endymion*. As on the 'Broad Fourteens' three weeks before, Weddigen snatched the opportunity. He fired a single torpedo which sank *Hawke* with the loss of 500 lives, virtually her entire complement.

Twenty-four hours after *Hawke* went down, the humiliation of 1 September was repeated in Scapa Flow. This time there were several 'periscope sightings' and one reported 'torpedo track' in the Flow. Out of its anchorage fled the Grand Fleet, not to return until 9 November. Jellicoe withdrew the Fleet to Lough Swilly in Northern Ireland—over 300 miles from where it would have been of any use if the High Seas Fleet had chosen to come out. 'We are hunted about the sea', lamented Commander Drax in the *Lion*, flagship of the battle-cruiser squadron, 'and have nowhere we can rest.' But the Grand Fleet's sense of nakedness began slowly to abate after its return to Scapa. Work on the base defences was now well advanced and on the 23rd *U-18*, attempting to creep into Scapa Flow,

was intercepted in Hoxa Sound by a trawler. Damaged by gunfire, *U-18* crawled out into the Pentland Firth but was forced to scuttle herself —a heartening reminder that the U-boats were not invulnerable. Month by month the defences were improved, and by 1915 the Grand Fleet was at last able to feel secure in its anchorage.

What remained, however, was the British fear of being lured within range of German submarines. This was shown during the Battle of the Dogger Bank (24 January 1915) when Admiral Beatty's battle-cruisers intercepted a weaker German battle-cruiser force under Admiral Hipper, and gave chase. At the height of the action, Beatty reported, 'submarines were reported on the starboard bow and I personally observed the wash of a torpedo two points on our starboard bow'. Beatty's instinctive reaction to this non-existent threat—there was not a U-boat within 60 miles—was to order his ships to swing sharply away to port, and Hipper's battle-cruisers escaped. The British had been granted the boon for which they had yearned since the outbreak of war—a fair crack at the High Seas Fleet, or even part of it—but their submarine neurosis had made them drop the catch.

Captain Johnson stands forlornly atop the capsized hull of his cruiser *Cressy*, torpedoed with *Hogue* and *Aboukir* on 22 September 1914. This was the only occasion in naval history when a submarine sank three enemy cruisers in a single hour.

34 /

Opposite: Artist's impression of the British submarine *B11* lounging on the surface after torpedoing the Turkish battleship *Messudieh* in the Dardanelles (13 December 1914). Actually, Lieutenant Holbrook added his victim after closing submerged to a range of 80 yards; he then watched her sink through his periscope. But this was only the prelude to *B11*'s epic retreat through the Dardanelles minefields—blind, due to instrument failure—which set a new record of nine hours submerged, remarkable for so small a boat.

By the time of the Dogger Bank action the potentialities of the submarine had already been demonstrated in the Mediterranean—this time by the British. Turkey had entered the war on the side of Germany and Austria-Hungary at the beginning of November. This added the blockade of Turkey to the task of keeping the Austro-Hungarian fleet safely bottled up in the Adriatic Sea. The most obvious point at which the French and British might exploit their superiority at sea and carry the war to the Turks was the Dardanelles. This narrow and crooked strait led directly to Constantinople and offered the chance of an Anglo-French link-up with the Russians in the Black Sea. Unfortunately this was just as obvious to the Turks and their German advisers. The Dardanelles were known to be densely mined and covered from either shore by emplaced guns. No conventional surface fleet could live in the Dardanelles and prospects of lone submarines running under the defences were highly questionable. But the British were the first to give it a try.

In late 1914 the only British submarines in the eastern Mediterranean were three small boats of the 'B' class. These were petrol-engined, of doubtful submerged endurance and lacking a gun with which to fight if forced to the surface. But on 13 December 1914 Lieutenant Norman Holbrook entered the mouth of the Dardanelles in *B11*. Despite the strong currents in the strait Holbrook managed to work *B11* past the lower minefields and approach Çanakkale (Chanak), the narrowest defile below the Sea of Marmara. Below Çanakkale he found the old Turkish battleship *Messudieh*, approached submerged to the point-blank range of 80 yards, and sank her. But on turning for home Holbrook ran into severe trouble. As on most early British submarines, *B11*'s compass was mounted outside the hull to prevent it from being affected by the submarine's residual magnetism; the compass card was viewed by the helmsman through lenses. But now these lenses became fogged with condensation. With no compass readings to steer by, Holbrook had no choice but to navigate by dead reckoning, guessing at his whereabouts by taking hasty surveys through the periscope. During her hazardous retreat, much of it spent bumping along the bottom, *B11* spent over nine hours submerged—a feat beyond all expectations for a boat of her size. When *B11* finally rejoined the fleet her battery was completely exhausted. For this fine achievement Holbrook got the VC, his first Lieutenant the DSO, and every man in the crew received the

DSC or the DSM, according to his rank. Hersing and Weddigen were the first submarine captains to sink enemy warships in the open sea, but Holbrook was the first to sink an enemy warship in waters theoretically safe from attack.

The year 1915 opened with another humiliation for the British in home waters, dispelling the fond belief still lingering in some quarters that the English Channel was somehow immune from penetration by U-boats. At 2.30 am on 1 January the pre-Dreadnought battleship *Formidable* was torpedoed and sunk by *U-24* off Start Point in the western Channel. This latest sinking came about largely because several British admirals, even after the painful lessons of the past few months, still considered the submarine to be an overrated weapon. (A similar phenomenon cropped up 25 years later at the outset of World War II, when some admirals obstinately held to the belief that a warship's guns automatically spelled defeat for air attacks. This myth was not finally dispelled until Japanese aircraft sunk the *Repulse* and *Prince of Wales* in December 1941.) One such diehard admiral at the end of 1914 was Sir Lewis Bayly, commanding the Channel Fleet. *Formidable* was lost when, as the rearmost ship in a squadron proceeding in neat line-ahead, she was steaming placidly along a dead straight course in bright moonlight at a leisurely ten knots, making no evasive movements whatsoever. For his serene complacency in neglecting even the most rudimentary anti-submarine precautions, Bayly was sacked from command of the Channel Fleet. It was a timely example, doubling as the Admiralty's official announcement that the old methods of waging war at sea could no longer be accepted as adequate.

There was just as much reluctance to accept this fact in Germany as there was in Britain. The German decision to wage submarine commerce warfare against Britain, taken in February 1915, was not a sudden, ruthless move by the German government. It had grown uncertainly from the unforeseen circumstances created by six months of a war which, so far from ending by Christmas, had produced an entrenched stalemate with no immediate solution in sight. As the German Armies in France and Belgium dug in to defend their gains, the role of the German Navy was automatically enhanced. The U-boat arm was clearly the only force capable of inflicting real damage on Britain's fleets—mercantile as well as naval.

Most of the German surface warships at large on the high seas in August 1914 had been rounded

up and sunk by January 1915, and the few survivors still eluding the Allied squadrons were living on borrowed time. Thus, by default, the task of attacking Britain's vital imports of war materials was bound to pass to the U-boats sooner or later. Between August 1914 and February 1915 their achievements against British commerce remained slight: only ten British merchantmen sunk since 13 October 1914, when *U-17* had stopped, searched and sunk the steamship *Glitra* off the Norwegian coast (following the provisions of International Law). But this insignificant performance by the U-boats was the result of the restrictions imposed on the submarine's *modus operandi* by the Hague Convention. If the U-boats could be allowed to attack merchantmen without warning, vastly different results could be achieved.

The most dramatic implication of unrestricted submarine warfare was its extension to merchantmen flying neutral flags as well as those flying the Red Ensign. To this Germany was able to retort that the Royal Navy's wartime insistence on its traditional 'right of search' of all vessels was itself a violation of International Law. Moreover, the wearing of neutral flags as a defensive measure was an age-old *ruse de guerre*. If the British continued to use neutral shipping to carry their war imports, and to advise their merchant skippers to fly neutral flags, Germany could hardly be expected to tolerate such a one-sided state of affairs.

The risk of a 'massacre of the innocents' among civilian women and children if passenger liners were attacked was another objection which the Germans were able to parry. The British themselves had involved passenger liners in the naval war by requisitioning such vessels as auxiliary merchant cruisers on the outbreak of war. Liners were also able to be used as troop carriers as well as to carry large quantities of war materials. No warship—surface vessel or submarine—could be expected to pass up such a target, and if civilians persisted in sailing in liners after due warning had been given they would have only themselves to blame.

Such, in outline, was the reasoning behind the first German attempt at a deliberate submarine campaign against British commerce, which duly opened on 18 February 1915 after the fortnight's warning had elapsed. It was certainly not an unrestricted campaign: ships flying neutral flags still had to be positively identified as hostile or in breach of the neutrality laws before they could be attacked. Nor were there anything like *enough* U-boats (only 22 in mid-

Oil bleeds into the sea as a merchantman sinks by the stern after a U-boat attack.

Above: Death of the *Lusitania*, the nightmare come true.
Right: American headlines above the bare-faced German statement that *Lusitania* 'was naturally armed with guns'.

February) to carry out an effective campaign. The time—four days—taken up in sailing out round the British Isles to reach a patrol area on Britain's Western Approaches, plus the time needed for repairs, maintenance and replenishment with stores and ammunition between patrols, meant that on average only four U-boats could stay on patrol at a time. For all that, the U-boats managed to sink 39 British merchant-men from 18 February to the end of April, during which period only four U-boats were lost.

The foremost casualty was Germany's first U-boat ace, Otto Weddigen, lost with his crew when *U-29* was sunk on 18 March. Weddigen, patrolling off the Moray Firth, caught a British battle squadron exercising at sea and attacked. But his opening torpedo missed the battleship

*Neptune* and an alert lookout spotted *U-29*'s periscope from *Dreadnought*. Beautifully handled, *Dreadnought* wheeled out of line, steered for the periscope's 'feather' of white water and trampled the U-boat under before Weddigen had had the chance to go deep. On his previous patrol Weddigen, who favoured surface attacks against merchantmen, had sunk six merchant ships in a single patrol and earned the nickname of the 'polite pirate' from the British. His death beneath the keel of an 18,000-ton battleship was not likely to encourage other U-boat captains to take liberties with 32,000-ton oceanliners.

The most notorious event of the new U-boat campaign was, of course, the sinking of the liner *Lusitania* in the early afternoon of 7 May, with the loss of 1201 men, women and children and a contingent of 128 American citizens. The culprit was *Kapitänleutnant* Walter Schwieger of *U-20*. On his last patrol in the North Sea, he had nursed his leaking U-boat home after having narrowly survived a ramming attack by a merchantman he had challenged on the surface. He saw no reason to spare *Lusitania*, which he knew to have been correctly warned of the existence of the German 'war zone' around Britain, and which he believed to be a potential troop-carrier and natural vehicle for war contraband. Stubborn official secrecy, extending to the British Admiralty and the White House in Washington, means that the precise nature of *Lusitania*'s cargo will probably never be known. But a large explosion—and not exploding

**The Weather**
Fair and somewhat cooler Sunday; Monday, fair; moderate southwest to west winds.

# New York American
THE TWENTIETH CENTURY NEWSPAPER

This Edition of THE AMERICAN consists of the following Sections:
1—Part I. 5—Editorial and Dramatic
2—Fore II—Sporting 6—"Billy" Sunday
    and Automobiles. 7—City Life.
3—Want Ads. 8—Magazine
4—Society. 9—comics.

No. 11,817.  ○ ○ ○  Copyright, 1915, by Star Company  SUNDAY  NEW YORK, MAY 9, 1915  SUNDAY  Registered in U. S. Patent Office  PRICE FIVE CENTS

## LUSITANIA DEAD 1,256---115 AMERICANS
## GERMANY OFFICIALLY ADMITS SINKING SHIP

### U.S. WILL ACT QUICKLY; DRASTIC STEPS URGED AS INDIGNATION RISES

Wilson Besieged with Telegrams and Situation Is Regarded as Most Momentous in Many Years—Gerard Cabled for Germany's Explanation

Washington, May 8.—The rising tide of popular indignation against the sinking of the Lusitania by a German submarine with its consequent enormous loss of life of American citizens has caused Administration officials to indicate more positive views for comprehensive action than was revealed by those officials earlier

### HUNDREDS MASSED ON DECK AS LINER REARED IN HER DEATH PLUNGE

Survivors Tell Thrilling Stories of Last Fateful Moments—Sixty Perish as Lifeboat Falls—Mothers Clasping Dead Babies Picked Up in Water

*Special Cable to International News Service.*
Queenstown, May 8.—Thrilling stories of the Lusitania disaster were told by survivors who landed here. F. J. Gauntlett, of New York, traveling in company with A. L. Hopkins, president of the Newport News Shipbuilding Co. (who is missing), and S. M. Knox, president of the New York Shipbuilding Co.,

### GERMANY'S OFFICIAL STATEMENT

Berlin, Via Wireless to London, May 9, 2:45 A. M. THE following official communication was issued to-night:

"*The Cunard liner Lusitania was yesterday torpedoed by a German submarine and sank.*

"*The Lusitania was naturally armed with guns, as were recently most of the English mercantile steamers. Moreover, as is well known here, she had large quantities of war material in her cargo.*

"*Her owners, therefore, knew to what danger the passengers were exposed. They alone bear all the responsibility for what has happened.*

"*Germany, on her part, left nothing undone to repeatedly and strongly warn them. The Imperial Ambassador in Washington even went so far as to make a public warning, so as to draw attention to this danger. The English press sneered then at the warning and relied on*

### FROHMAN'S BODY IS FOUND; VANDERBILT AND HUBBARD LOST

● London, May 8.—The first list of identified dead in the Lusitania disaster was given out here this afternoon. The bodies of the following persons have been recovered and positively identified, and are being embalmed:
DR. F. S. PEARSON, of New York.
MRS. AMELIA McDONALD.
PATRICK CALLON.
ARTHUR FOLEY.
Other identified Americans dead are

boilers—blew open her forward hull and took her to the bottom in 18 minutes. This can hardly be attributed to the destructive effect of *U-20*'s torpedoes. Only the previous day Schwieger had torpedoed two Harrison Line steamers, *Candidate* and *Centurion*. *Candidate* only sank after two hours when Schwieger perforated her hull at the waterline with shellfire; *Centurion* suffered two torpedoes and still took 80 minutes to sink.

With *Lusitania* the tragic loss of life was boosted by the ship's rapid list, confusion among the passengers and safety provisions which would be considered grossly inadequate by modern standards. Allied propaganda had a field day with the 'massacre' of women and children, omitting any sustained comment on the fact that the victims' menfolk had deliberately taken a dangerous risk. There was even less eagerness to admit that the British Admiralty had not exactly exerted itself in providing an escort through the war zone for *Lusitania*. Over 48 hours before *Lusitania* was hit, the Admiralty had known that U-boats were operating off southern Ireland. But the light cruiser *Juno*, originally detailed to rendezvous with *Lusitania* west of Fastnet, had been ordered back to Queenstown because of her 'unsuitability' to meet submarine attack—without Captain Turner of the *Lusitania* being told. Had *Lusitania* come within Schwieger's periscope view with *Juno* in attendance it would probably have been a different story. *Lusitania* was far too big a ship to be zig-zagged at 20 knots—certainly not with fare-paying passengers on board, whose custom the Cunard Company hoped to keep.

Though the *Lusitania* incident did not bring the United States into the war, repeated German sinkings of ships carrying American citizens continued to incense American public opinion and worry the Kaiser's statesmen. After *U-24* sank the British steamer *Arabic* on 19 August, killing three Americans, Washington's protest was so sharp that diplomatic caution prevailed in Germany. A new order went out on 30 August: passenger steamers were no longer to be attacked by submerged submarines, or without warning having been given and passengers and crew safely taken off. With the U-boats thus obliged once more to expose themselves on the surface, the inevitable result was the suspension of the campaign. Three weeks later, on 18 September, all U-boats were ordered to be withdrawn from the English Channel and Western Approaches.

All in all, the first German submarine cam-

paign of February–September 1915 deserves to rank with Bonaparte's Italian campaign of 1796–97, or the debut of Guderian's Panzers in the Polish campaign of September 1939, as one of the most prominent milestones in the history of modern warfare. It saw the submarine come of age as the first modern weapon to make war a universal scourge, rather than a professional duel between rival armies and fleets. In the short term nothing decisive was accomplished: the British built more merchant ships than they lost, and the Germans built more U-boats than *they* lost. But in the long term the first U-boat offensive was, beyond question, a completely successful experiment. In 1915 U-boats destroyed 748,000 tons of British merchant shipping, a monthly average of over 62,333 tons and an increase of over a hundredfold on the meagre 600 tons sunk per month between August and December 1914. Given all the restrictions under which the U-boats had to operate in 1915, this was an unanswerable demonstration of the potential of the submarine and the efficacy of undersea commerce war. By January 1916 Admiral von Holtzendorff, Chief of the German Naval Staff, was able to inform Chancellor Bethmann Hollweg that 'If after the winter season, that is to say under suitable weather conditions, the economic war by submarines be begun again with every means available and without restrictions which from the outset must cripple its effectiveness, a defi-

nite prospect may be held out that, judged by previous experience, British resistance will be broken in six months at the outside.'

In 1915 the U-boat arm had gained all the salient knowledge to allow such a confident prediction to be made. Perhaps the most im-portant lesson was the immense value of a deck gun which, when fired at a victim's waterline, was a far more economical way of sinking ships than the costly torpedo. Gun ammunition also took up less stowage space than torpedoes (only eight of which could be carried) and allowed U-boats to stay longer on patrol. The Germans also used the 1915 campaign to diversify the U-boat arm and try out their small coastal U-boats, the 'UB' class, originally armed only with two bow torpedo tubes. These boats were small enough to be shipped in sections by rail and assembled at the Austrian port of Pola, to operate against the Allies in the Adriatic. Also introduced in 1915 was the 'UC' class of mine-laying submarine, the first 15 boats armed with nothing heavier than a machine gun and carrying 12 mines in six vertical launching-tubes. (German mines accounted for 77,000 tons of British shipping in 1915.) The 'UB' and 'UC' boats made up the Flanders Flotilla based at Bruges close to the British coastal shipping lanes; it was formed on 29 March. In August 1915, the most effective month of the campaign, the Germans had 13 boats of all classes at sea and pushed British merchant shipping losses up to a record 148,400 tons.

The factor which proved of greatest assistance to the Germans in their first U-boat campaign was the complete failure of the British to develop

'We live again'—fanciful depiction of German submariners cheering as the periscope of a hunting British submarine passes close alongside. Such episodes were inevitable until submarines were fitted with sound-detecting hydrophones.

anti-submarine weapons and tactics. Lacking the means to detect submerged submarines, they nevertheless tried to take the offensive against the U-boats without realising that they were relying on the enemy making mistakes—never the safest of assumptions in war. The British tried to seal off the Dover Straits with a vast barrage of anti-submarine minefields and nets, the idea being that a snagged U-boat would trigger an indicator buoy, reveal its presence and be smashed as it lay helpless. For U-boats which escaped the British mines, the explosive sweep—a charge towed beneath the surface—was brought into service at the end of 1914, but the nets could be by-passed via their gaps, dived under or pierced; the minefields were a joke. British mines tended either not to explode when hit, or to drift from their laid positions. Only three U-boats (*U-5*, *U-11* and *U-37*) were sunk by mines in the Dover Straits and English Channel between August 1914 and December 1915. The explosive sweep was a marginally better idea, but was only of any use when a U-boat or periscope was actually sighted and the surface patrols given some idea of their quarry's course. *U-8*, sunk on 4 March 1915, was the only boat sunk by explosive sweeps in the Dover Straits in 1915.

The decoy or 'Q-ship', an innocent-looking vessel armed with concealed guns for the discomfiture of U-boats attacking on the surface, was a typical British half-measure in 1915. Q-ships accounted for three U-boats towards the end of the campaign—*U-36* in July, *U-27* in August, *U-41* in September—but once the

Demonstration of hydrophone positioning from a flying-boat's cockpit.

C R Fleming-Williams' painting of flying-boats attacking a U-boat, crippled and unable to dive.

Germans learned of their employment U-boat captains naturally tended to be wary. Indeed, so far from countering the U-boat menace, Q-ships helped increase it by strengthening the German case for a completely unrestricted offensive. Down to the end of the war Q-ships sank or helped sink 14 U-boats—but 31 Q-ships were lost in the process, torpedoed by U-boat skippers determined to take no chances. Another more cumbersome and elaborate half-measure was a British decoy towing a submerged submarine, communicating with the latter by telephone. Once a U-boat was sighted the British submarine would slip its tow and ambush the U-boat. Using this method the British submarine *C24* managed to sink *U-40* off Aberdeen in June 1915; but as with the Q-ship tactic, the danger of towed British submarines only encouraged U-boats to torpedo likely-looking fishing boats, especially if they seemed to be towing something.

But the real problem, perfectly summed up by Arthur J Marder in *From the Dreadnought to Scapa Flow*, was the British Admiralty's failure to diagnose the threat correctly:

'There was, at the Admiralty and afloat, altogether too much talk about "offensive action" against U-boats and far too little thought given to what was meant by "offensive action". What was, in effect, meant was trying to mine and bomb the U-boats in their bases, and, above all, to hunt them to destruction at sea. None of these measures was successful. The dogma "Seek out and destroy the enemy" governed all activities and precluded rational action. While the main difficulty with hunting tactics at this time was the lack of efficient submarine detectors of submerged submarines, the strategy of hunting was fundamentally unsound; it left the initiative to the elusive enemy. As a consequence, hunting became a succession of futile follow-up operations after U-boats had achieved successful attacks in a diversity of places. . . . The so-called hunting of submarines was a waste of effort and of resources except very infrequently when luck intervened and a U-boat captain made a mess of things. Indicator nets used in narrow waters were an attempt to overcome the problem of under-water detection of submarines, but they had severe limitations and were often disappointing.

'In the event, it was "defensive measures" such as the arming and routing of merchant-

men which proved much more successful in curbing the U-boats' successes, but what, eventually and decisively, defeated them was the so-called 'defensive' measure of convoy. This was because it concentrated the main anti-submarine effort where it was most likely to be effectual.'

The British failure to assign top-priority status to the U-boat menace in early 1915 is partly explained by the fact that the campaign opened as the Allies were preparing for their own assault on the Dardanelles, first with warships alone (February/March) and then with large-scale troop landings on the Gallipoli peninsula (April). The strategic implications of the Dardanelles venture were not missed by the Germans; nor was the ensuing concentration of Allied naval units and shipping in the eastern Mediterranean, which in 1915 became the target for a parallel U-boat offensive.

Germany had already pledged U-boat reinforcements for her ally Austria, in the form of 'UB' class boats sent overland in sections to Pola. *UB-1* and *UB-15* eventually joined the Austrian Navy as *U-10* and *U-11*, and five more of the first 17 'UB' boats completed in 1915 went to Pola. But the German Admiralty also decided to send the big seagoing U-boats into the Mediterranean to help the Turks hold Gallipoli.

On 25 April, the day of the British landings on Gallipoli, Otto Hersing sailed from Germany in *U-21*, and after refuelling and repairing at Pola arrived off Gallipoli on 25 May. There he found targets galore. The British warships swarming off the beaches, trying to give fire support to the wretched troops ashore, had heard that U-boats were on their way out to the Mediterranean and were already gripped by the same U-boat neurosis which had swept the Grand Fleet in the first months of the war. But apart from the deployment of anti-torpedo nets on the ships and much aimless steaming to and fro, there were if anything even less effective anti-submarine measures than in home waters. Hersing had bad luck with his first three torpedoes, which missed the Russian cruiser *Askold* and the British battleships *Swiftsure* and *Vengeance*. He then spent two hours stalking the battleship *Triumph*, chose his moment well and sent her to the bottom with a single torpedo.

Though *U-21*'s periscope was sighted by the aghast onlookers ashore, Hersing evaded his disorganised naval pursuers and lay on the bottom for 28 hours until forced to surface and

British submarine *E14* bound for the Dardanelles, leaves Mudros with Commander Boyle (in overcoat) on the bridge.

recharge batteries by night. On the 27th he sighted the battleship *Majestic* with her torpedo nets out and a host of small patrol boats in attendance. Once again Hersing waited for an unimpeded shot, then fired a single torpedo which went clean through *Majestic*'s net and sank her. The result of this second sinking was momentous: all Allied capital ships were promptly withdrawn to the island of Lemnos, depriving the troops on Gallipoli of heavy-calibre fire support from the sea. Even if, by some miracle, the troops had broken through the Turkish defences on Gallipoli, the U-boat fear implanted by Hersing's arrival would have prevented the Allied fleet from lying close

enough to the Dardanelles to cover the clearing of the Turkish minefields inside, then advancing in support of the land forces.

Following the exploit of *B11* back in December 1914, British submarines spearheaded the assault on the Dardanelles by forcing the straits submerged and emerging into the Sea of Marmara. The Australian Navy was the first to make it, when Lieutenant-Commander H D Stoker and *AE2* broke through into the Marmara on 26 April having sunk a Turkish gunboat *en route*. He was followed within 48 hours by Lieutenant-Commander E C Boyle in *E14*. *AE2* fell victim to a Turkish torpedo-boat on 29 April but Boyle ran amok with his tor-

Top: The crew of HMS *Grampus* cheer *E11* (Nasmith) as she emerges from the Dardanelles. Above: Master weapon in the Marmara, essential for 'all-round' raiding—the gun of submarine *E2*.

pedoes, destroying Turkish troop and ammunition transports. *E14* lingered in the Marmara for a week after her last torpedo had been fired, preventing any Turkish transports from crossing to Gallipoli by the mere threat of her presence.

The third British boat to penetrate the Marmara was *E11* (Lieutenant-Commander M E Dunbar Nasmith), who set out on her mission on 18 May. Nasmith's exploits on this cruise made him a legend in the British submarine service. Once in the Marmara he started by capturing a small *dhow* which he used as mobile camouflage, lashing *E11* alongside, trimmed down and virtually invisible. After sinking a gunboat and a transport loaded with guns, gun mountings and ammunition, Nasmith chased a third transport into the port of Rodosto and sank her as she tied up to the quay, then forced a fourth victim to run ashore before making good his escape. Nasmith's

most famous feat was penetrating Constantinople roads and sinking the transport *Stamboul* as she lay at the wharfside embarking stores. Frustrated, like Stoker and Boyle before him, by *E11*'s lack of a gun, Nasmith developed an extremely hazardous technique for eking out his dwindling stock of torpedoes. Each torpedo was set to float at the end of its run. If a torpedo missed, Nasmith would track it down, then personally swim across and unscrew the firing pistol from the warhead. The torpedo would then be guided back into *E11*'s stern tube and prepared for another shot.

Both Boyle and Nasmith (each of whom won the VC) returned to the Marmara after their boats had gone to Malta to have guns fitted. This improvement made to the five submarines which operated in the Marmara throughout the later months of 1915 reduced Turkish seaborne traffic to *dhows* and forced the Turks to withdraw all their surviving warships to the Black

Sea. Inevitably, there were casualties. *E7* was caught and destroyed in the strengthened net defences of the Dardanelles on 4 September; *E20* was ambushed and sunk by the newly arrived German submarine *UB-14* on 21 October 1914.

For all their tactical brilliance, the British submarines in the Marmara achieved little of strategic value. Germany's submarine build-up in the southern theatre from August 1915 proved capable of snatching the initiative in the Mediterranean even before the British evacuated Gallipoli in December 1915–January 1916. Hersing moved up to Varna on the Black Sea coast and was reinforced with 'UB' and 'UC' boats to operate against the Russians in the Black Sea and the British in the Marmara. (*UB-14*'s sinking of *E20* was one of the first successes of Hersing's half-flotilla.) In August 1915 four more U-boats—*U-33*, *U-34*, *U-35* and *U-39*, with *U-38* joining in November—were sent to the Adriatic to operate from Cattaro against Anglo-French shipping in the Mediterranean. And it was one of the latter, *U-35*, which

became the most successful submarine of all time under command of the U-boat 'ace of aces', Lothar Arnauld de la Perière.

From the time she commissioned in November 1914 to the Armistice four years later, *U-35* sank 224 merchant ships totalling 535,900 tons. Of these, over 83 percent—189 ships, totalling 446,708 tons—were sunk between November 1915 and March 1918, when Arnauld de la Perière commanded *U-35*. His record month was 26 July–20 August 1916, when he sank 54 ships totalling 91,000 tons. But Arnauld de la Perière's achievement did not depend on the use of the submarine as an undersea weapon. It was, rather, the masterly exploitation of the contemporary *weaknesses* of the submarine as a weapons system. If Arnauld de la Perière had relied on submerged torpedo attacks his count of victims could never have mounted so spectacularly. But he was an exponent of the careful periscope reconnaissance followed by a sudden gun action on the surface. Brilliant loner that he was, he handled *U-35* as a submersible surface raider. And he was most

Below: A U-boat takes on more shells between cruises.

48 /

generously assisted by the failure of the Allies to devise a sane anti-submarine programme. Instead the French and British persisted in sailing merchantmen along fixed routes, escorted by warships whose responsibility for their charges ended abruptly on the boundary of each command zone. There were 18 such zones, each one jealously autonomous and indifferent to its neighbours' fortunes. It was easy for the U-boats to dodge the scattered patrols, and the situation remained so until the Allies belatedly came to their senses and began to sail their ships in protective convoys.

The Germans began 1916 with 58 operational U-boats and a wealth of most promising experience. As the British still had no effective anti-submarine weapons or tactics this was the moment, hindsight argues, when Germany should have taken the plunge and staked all on an unrestricted U-boat campaign. But Bethmann Hollweg still feared that such a move, with the inevitable American casualties it would inflict, would goad the United States into joining the Allies. For 1916—as they had done in August 1914 and would do again in March 1918—the Germans put their faith in a land offensive, the objective in 1916 being to 'bleed the French Army white' at Verdun. Once the French had been rendered incapable of further effort, 'that breaking point would be reached and England's best sword knocked out of her hand'. To accompany the Verdun offensive, which opened on 21 February 1916, the U-boat campaign against Britain was resumed, but carefully. In an absurd compromise, the undersea war was to be simultaneously intensified and held in check.

The instructions to U-boats issued on 13 March ordered that all merchantmen encountered in the war zone were to be sunk, and those encountered outside to be sunk only if they were armed. Passenger steamers (armed or not) were not to be attacked by submerged submarines—which, in practice, meant not at all. Briefly, British merchant shipping losses soared again, with 37 ships (126,000 tons) sunk in April. By June 1916 British merchant-ship losses had fallen off to 16 ships (36,000 tons) for the month. But the summer of 1916 was the last time that the British Admiralty was able to cling to the delusion that the fall-off in sinkings was due to defensive measures. From September the submarine campaign began again, and this time it would not be suspended but would escalate into the unrestricted offensive for which the U-boat protagonists had never ceased to

agitate. Their campaign began.

As 1917 opened, the year in which the U-boats would come closer to defeating Britain than any element of the German armed forces was to do in either of the world wars, the deadly statistics for the world's first unrestricted submarine campaign had already been drafted. They all revolved round tonnage—the tonnage of merchant ships which the British must keep flowing in order to stay in the war—and the number of operational U-boats available to sink it. If the U-boats sank more merchant tonnage than the German Navy lost U-boats, the British were bound to lose. Conversely, if the British could preserve (or replace) enough merchant tonnage, and sink enough U-boats in the process, they would survive—and so would the grinding blockade being inflicted on Germany, which the German High Command knew full well was bound to strangle the German war effort if not thrown off.

The U-boats came close to victory because the British took so long in deciding to sail their merchant ships in convoy and to mass-produce depth-charges—the deadliest anti-submarine weapon produced in World War I.

The British survived because the Germans had based their calculations on the ease of sinking large numbers of independently routed merchantmen, but had developed no tactics for systematic attacks on convoys.

At the beginning of 1917, the Germans had 138 U-boats in commission, including 'UB' and 'UC' types. During the unrestricted campaign, which opened on 1 February, only about 40 would be at sea on any given day and half of those would be heading home for repairs and replenishment. (The monthly average number at sea between August 1914 and January 1917 had been 12.) But given the Allied shipping weaknesses which prevailed until the adoption of convoy, there were enough U-boats to inflict the following losses on the British alone:

| 1917 (month) | Ships sunk (British) | Tons |
|---|---|---|
| January | 35 | 109,954 |
| February | 86 | 256,394 |
| March | 103 | 283,647 |
| April | 155 | 516,394 |

As the U-boat offensive was accompanied by a stepped-up mining programme and the efforts of three elusive surface raiders disguised as merchantmen, British shipping losses were, by the end of April, fast approaching the monthly

level which the Germans had calculated would guarantee Britain's collapse. The German objective was the sinking of 600,000 tons per month and the permanent frightening-off of the 1,200,000 tons of neutral shipping on which the Allies depended. But, as tends to happen with issues of such magnitude and novelty, both sides got their sums wrong.

The main reason why the British delayed their vital adoption of the convoy system until May 1917 was that the Admiralty believed it to be an impossible task. This negative attitude was erroneously based on a set of figures which suggested that there were far too many merchantmen at sea on any given day to be sailed and escorted in convoy. These were the customs returns, which showed the coming and going of vessels of every nationality over 100 tons—many of which, coasters and cross-Channel streamers, were counted several times per week. But the figure that mattered was the amount of ocean-going steamers over 1000 tons arriving and departing every week. Not until early April was it revealed that there were only about 140 of such ships, coming and going, 280 in all—not 5000-odd.

The Admiralty only had a few weeks to digest

this radically different prospect before Prime Minister Lloyd George, breathing fire and insisting that the convoy strategy be adopted at once, descended on the Admiralty on 30 April 1917. Though this must be accounted one of the most timely political interventions in naval history, Lloyd George was not solely responsible for the adoption of the convoy system: he merely gave the spur to the reversal of over two and a half years of opposition, born of rigid bureaucracy inside the Admiralty and failure to define the problem correctly.

The Germans were equally let down by their own miscalculations. Though they accepted that unrestricted U-boat warfare would probably bring in the Americans on the Allied side (as it did on 6 April 1917), they also believed that the United States had little of any immediate military value to contribute, and that the Allies could be forced into a negotiated peace before the United States was fully geared up for war. Above all the Germans believed that neutral countries would be permanently deterred from sailing cargoes to British ports. This did not happen. After six months—by which time the Germans had calculated that the British would be at their breaking-point—neutral shipping to

The first weapon in the counterattack against submerged submarines was the hydrophone, here shown in use on the British trawler *Thrive*. But without sonar to confirm range and bearing, all the hydrophone could do was to notify escort vessels when there were engine noises where no engine noises ought to be.

Below: *Wasserbomb!* An
American destroyer carries
out a depth-charge attack.
Opposite: *U-22* demon-
strates that submarines are
no less vulnerable to mines
than surface craft. When
she had her stern blown off
by a mine in April 1917,
*U-22* was lucky that the
explosion did not detonate
the warheads of the
torpedoes in her two stern
tubes (centre) or of the two
reloads (outboard).

Britain was back at 80 percent of its normal
volume and the British had rushed through a
totally new programme of shipping construction
and dockyard repairs—another feature of earlier
complacency and neglect for whose correction
the Germans had not bargained.

Moreover, the Germans believed that they
were sinking far more tonnage than they actually
were. This was due primarily to human error
on the part of the U-boat captains who, under
the immense stress of the campaign, tended to
over-estimate the tonnage of their victims (just
as, in 1940, RAF Fighter Command pilots were
to over-estimate the numbers of German aircraft they shot down). But the biggest error on
the German side was the failure to guess how
quickly the Allies could reorganise their hither-
to vulnerable shipping, and present the U-boats
with the insuperable problem of escorted
convoys.

The adoption of the convoy principle swept
merchantmen together into formation; the
scrapping of the futile 'anti-submarine patrols',
which the U-boats had always found so easy
to dodge, provided the convoy's escort warships. Now, instead of picking off isolated
victims one by one, U-boats had to hunt for
these big defensive formations in order to
maintain their tonnage quotas. Here British
radio interception proved invaluable. A U-boat
reporting its position to base would be 'over-
heard' in London; the convoy commodore
would be alerted and the convoy swung away
from the ambush which seemed to be preparing.
For U-boats which did make contact with
convoys, keeping in touch imposed terrific
strain on the crews and every attack invited an
instant counterattack by the escorts.

Painfully developed throughout 1915 and
distributed in tiny numbers from early 1916,
the depth-charge was a bomb fired by a hydro-
static detonator, which operated as soon as the
charge had sunk to a pre-selected depth. A near-

miss could destroy a U-boat, and anything between about 14 and 28 feet usually caused so much damage that the U-boat would be forced to surface. The strain of awaiting a depth-charge attack, as the noise of the hunter's screws welled to crescendo and passed overhead, followed by the thunderous concussion of the charges, had to be repeatedly endured as the U-boats strove to come to grips with the convoys. This was grimly summed up by future U-boat supremo Karl Dönitz, whose last World War I command (in the Mediterranean, where convoy was also introduced) was *U-68*:

'The oceans at once became bare and empty; for long periods at a time the U-boats, operating individually, would see nothing at all; and then, suddenly, up would loom a huge concourse of ships, thirty or fifty or more of them, surrounded by an escort of warships of all types. The solitary U-boat, which most probably had sighted the convoy purely by chance, would then attack, thrusting again and again and persisting, if the commander had strong nerves, for perhaps several days and nights, until the physical exhaustion of both commander and crew called a halt. The lone U-boat might well sink

one or two of the ships, or even several, but that was a poor percentage of the whole.'

Though the first experimental convoys started to run in May 1917 it took another two months before any genuine easement was felt; but the fall-off in losses to U-boat attack from the terrible April of 1917 tells its own story:

| 1917 (month) | Ships sunk (British) | Tons |
|---|---|---|
| April | 155 | 516,394 |
| May | 106 | 320,572 |
| June | 116 | 417,925 |
| July | 88 | 319,931 |
| August | 84 | 310,551 |
| September | 68 | 173,437 |
| October | 79 | 261,649 |
| November | 56 | 154,806 |

Thus within six months of the slaughter inflicted in April 1917, the U-boats were already sinking 50 percent less tonnage and their unrestricted campaign had clearly failed to knock Britain out of the war. The new Atlantic convoys were not as big as Dönitz so gloomily claimed; the largest, sailed in June 1918, numbered 47 ships and the average size was in the region of 20–25 ships. But the convoys *did* sweep most of the easy victims off the sealanes, driving the U-boats closer and closer inshore. Down to July 1917 55 percent of sinkings had taken place over 50 miles from land; by December 1917 this had fallen off to eight percent. Altogether—from May 1917 to the Armistice in November 1918—16,070 ships sailed in ocean convoys and only 96 were sunk by U-boats: a mere 0.6 percent. When convoy was extended into British coastal and inshore waters in 1918 the results were even more gratifying: 0.24 percent sunk, or only 161 out of 67,888 ships convoyed in coastal waters down to the Armistice.

Part of the reason for the baffling of the U-boats was the fact that escort warships were always on hand to 'chase down' any U-boat which tried to attack a convoy. But the biggest virtue of convoy was that it prevented U-boats from doing what they had always had to do in order to make sure of a sinking: finish off their victims on the surface, either with gunfire or by boarding and placing explosive charges. A torpedoed ship now had an excellent chance of being taken in tow and brought safely to port, where improved repair facilities were waiting to send the stricken vessel quickly back to sea. Meanwhile, as likely as not, the U-boat com-

Above: *Deutschland* dressed overall for her American cruise.
A ticklish moment aboard *U-35*. Swaying over a replacement torpedo before easing its ungainly bulk down through the submarine's fore-hatch was a job which, if carried out at sea, as here, definitely called for calm seas and a steady boat.

of new boats and in some months actually surpassing it. In November and December 1917, for instance, 16 U-boats were lost and only 11 new ones were commissioned.

The defeat of the U-boats in 1917, however, was primarily due to the strictly defensive measure of convoy—not to any new Allied weaponry or tactics, or to the rising losses being inflicted on the U-boat arm.

Though the battle was confined mainly to the eastern Atlantic, Britain's Western Approaches and the Mediterranean, the Germans made one innovation which boded ill for the future. This was the deployment of long-range submarines capable of cruising to the American coast and back: the spectacular, outsize 'U-cruisers', displacing over 1500 tons and armed with a brace of 5.9-inch guns as well as bow torpedo tubes.

mander would have gone home claiming a torpedo hit and probable sinking—if he survived. Though U-boat losses never rose so high as to force a suspension of operations—as they were to do in the summer of 1943—more and more boats were being lost by the end of 1917. Sixty-five U-boats were sunk that year, 44 of them between July and December. By the end of the year, for the first time in the war, U-boat losses were approaching the construction rate

The U-cruisers were developed from the submarine merchantmen produced as an experimental counter to the British blockade, the first of which, *Deutschland*, made two propaganda trading voyages to the United States in 1916. When converted and armed as *U-155*, *Deutschland* made a maiden war cruise lasting

from 24 May to 4 September 1917 in which she sank ten steamers and seven sailing ships—nearly 52,000 tons of British, Allied and neutral shipping. Six others were converted and rushed into service, and over 30 more were ordered (thus adding considerably to the production problems of the more proven types). But the U-cruisers, like Arnauld de la Perière's *U-35*, were really a demonstration of the tactical weaknesses of World War I submarines: they were intended to intimidate and crush resistance *on the surface*, using gun-power. Operating alone they could never succeed in breaking up a convoy into defenceless individuals. Their initial successes came in the early days of the convoy system, before American participation enabled convoys to be run all the way across the Atlantic with adequate warship escort.

The shape of things to come was glimpsed by Hermann Bauer, commander of the U-boat arm since the beginning of the war. He suggested using the U-cruisers as command and supply ships for combined submarine attacks on the convoys, guiding U-boats to the target by radio in liaison with shore headquarters. This was overruled as far as U-cruiser operations were concerned, and although experiments in U-boat co-ordination were made it was found that radio communication was still too primitive to give the idea a fair trial. Bauer, who had done a magnificent job as commander of the U-boat arm since 1914, was replaced by *Kommodore* Andreas Michelsen in June 1917. Individual U-boat commanders, however, did pioneer the tactic of combined submarine attack, most notably Karl Dönitz in *U-68*. On 4 October 1918 *U-68* and *U-48* were pressing home an attack on a Mediterranean convoy when *U-68* was so badly damaged that Dönitz had to scuttle her and surrender. But this personal failure and humiliation did not persuade him that combined attack—*rudeltaktik*, or the 'wolf pack' concept—was a mistaken idea. In World War II he was to perfect it with deadly effect.

By the spring of 1918 the U-boats were still enough of a menace for the British to make their famous attempt to seal off the Bruges canal at Zeebrugge with blockships (22–23 April), in an attempt to curtail the operations of the Flanders Flotilla. Despite the high gallantry of the attackers the little 'UB' class boats were still able to squeeze past the blockships. The U-boat arm, numbering 123 operational boats at the beginning of the year, lost another 83 before the Armistice while only 80 new boats were completed. But the dedication of the German sub-

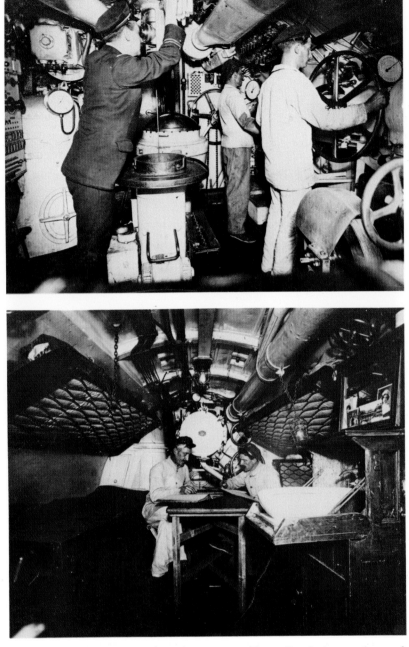

mariners, right to the last, was demonstrated by the exploit of *UB-116* (*Kapitänleutnant* Kurt Emsmann), barely three weeks before the Armistice.

In late October 1918 Emsmann embarked on a lone mission to penetrate Scapa Flow, a desperate attempt to prove that the German Navy still had teeth, and so improve Germany's bargaining position during the armistice negotiations. It was a grim demonstration of how much things had changed at Scapa since the panicky days of 1914. The Flow was now ringed with electrically triggered minefields, hydrophones and magnetic detectors to indicate when a submarine was passing over the mines. As Emsmann took *UB-116* into Hoxa Sound on the night of 28 October, the sound of his electric motors was picked up by the shore hydrophones; the needle on the observer's dial

Top: In the control room of the French submarine *Andromaque*. Beneath the periscope is the well into which the instrument descends when lowered. Above: Spacious crew quarters in the *Montgolfier*.

Gun armament proceeds
from the sublime to the
ridiculous. Left: *D4*, the
first British submarine to
carry a gun. Below and
right: The 'submarine
monitor' *M1*, with her
monstrous 12-inch gun.

flickered as *UB-116* crossed a controlled mine-field; a switch was thrown and a row of exploding mines sank *UB-116* with all hands.

When the world's first undersea war ended with the Armistice on 11 November 1918, all the indications were that the Allies had learned more in defence than the Germans had learned in attack. Convoy was the foundation of survival, with the massed merchantmen escorted by warships on the surface and, where possible, by aeroplanes and airships aloft. The mass production and distribution of depth-charges had enabled the escorts to counterattack with mounting effectiveness. Above all the ASDIC—the Anglo-French 'Anti-Submarine Detection Investigation Committee'—was already working flat out on the vital problem of detecting submerged submarines, the most important missing piece of the puzzle.

Had the war continued, the Germans would have begun the 1919 campaign with no real answer to the convoy problem. Though 185 U-boats were surrendered intact to the Allies and another 192 had been sunk or scuttled, far too many of them were of the U-cruiser type with its inherent emphasis on surface attack. In the field of 'artificial aids', the most important German discovery had been the value of hydrophones in detecting the approach of surface vessels, and the efficacy of 'silent routine' in foiling hydrophones listening from the noisy surface of the sea. There was little to choose between Allied and German submariners when it came to courage and endurance. But it was the

Above and below: The U-boats surrender. The Germans never learned that an upside-down 'lucky horseshoe' lets the luck run out.

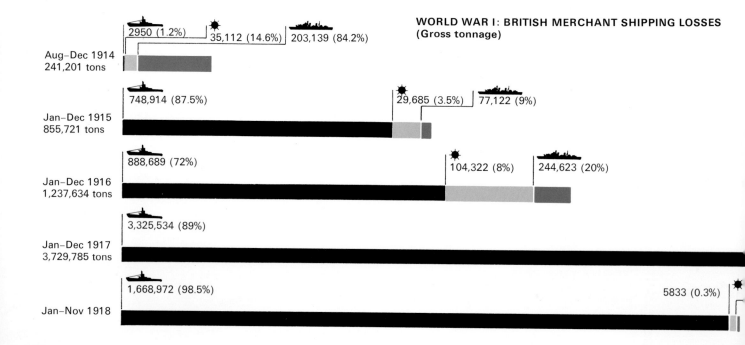

WORLD WAR I: BRITISH MERCHANT SHIPPING LOSSES
(Gross tonnage)

Aug–Dec 1914
241,201 tons
2950 (1.2%)  35,112 (14.6%)  203,139 (84.2%)

Jan–Dec 1915
855,721 tons
748,914 (87.5%)  29,685 (3.5%)  77,122 (9%)

Jan–Dec 1916
1,237,634 tons
888,689 (72%)  104,322 (8%)  244,623 (20%)

Jan–Dec 1917
3,729,785 tons
3,325,534 (89%)

Jan–Nov 1918
1,668,972 (98.5%)  5833 (0.3%)

# WORLD WAR I: U-BOAT CONSTRUCTION AND LOSSES

| 1914 | August |
| | September |
| | October |
| | November |
| | December |

| 1915 | January |
| | February |
| | March |
| | April |
| | May |
| | June |
| | July |
| | August |
| | September |
| | October |
| | November |
| | December |

| 1916 | January |
| | February |
| | March |
| | April |
| | May |
| | June |
| | July |
| | August |
| | September |
| | October |
| | November |
| | December |

| 1917 | January |
| | February |
| | March |
| | April |
| | May |
| | June |
| | July |
| | August |
| | September |
| | October |
| | November |
| | December |

| 1918 | January |
| | February |
| | March |
| | April |
| | May |
| | June |
| | July |
| | August |
| | September |
| | October– |
| | 11 November |

Sea- and Ocean-going types
(including Type C Minelayers)

Launched

Lost

Type B Coastal boats

Launched

Lost

Total U-boats operational
at the outbreak of war
(4th August 1914)—20

Grand total of U-boats
(all types) operational
from August 1914 to
November 1918—364

Grand total of U-boats
sunk (all types)—186

U-boats surrendered or
scuttled—178

U-boats planned for 1919
but scrapped or cancelled
—438

U-boats

Mines

Surface warships and aircraft

107,635 (3%)    296,616 (8%)

19,944 (1.1%)

British 'K-ship' (*K2*), one of the most remarkable craft produced in World War I. Steam turbines gave them an impressive surface speed of 24 knots, but a flared clipper bow was needed to prevent the bow being driven under.

German submarine arm which had introduced unrestricted submarine commerce war, proving the latter to be as deadly a potential war-winner as has ever been devised.

Literally the biggest phenomenon of World War I submarine development was the big submarine cruiser, designed for long-range patrols lasting a couple of months or more. This, the forerunner of the modern nuclear submarine, was inadequate in 1916–18 only in that its contemporary weaponry and machinery kept it shackled to the surface. The British experimented with submarine cruisers—the wartime 'K' ships and later 'M' class submarine monitors, the latter preposterously armed with a single 12-inch gun each. But all these proved was that large submarines were feasible; the experience of World War I had proved that submarines should not be tied down or made to manoeuvre as part of a surface fleet. Tactically, the submarine cruiser was a waste; it could do nothing that surface ships could not do better except

submerge, thus rendering its dominant (gun) weapons useless. The British sensibly abandoned submarine cruisers after *M1* sank in a Channel collision in 1925 and *M2* foundered in 1932; but the French went on to complete *Surcouf*, then the world's biggest submarine, in 1934. Though designed as a merchant raider, she proved in World War II to have no fully effective role.

Another fruit of World War I submarine development years ahead of its time was the specialised anti-submarine submarine—the type known today as the 'hunter-killer'. Operating as they were from the defensive, the British introduced the 'hunter-killer' in 1918, in the form of the 'R' class boats. Highly streamlined, the 'R' boats were the first submarines capable of greater speeds submerged (15 knots) than when surfaced (9.5 knots). They were not to be surpassed until the German Type XXI boats at the end of World War II. Between the wars, submarine development inevitably suffered from

and 250 submarines—scheduled for completion between 1944 and 1948.

The outbreak of war in 1939 bore no comparison to that of 1914, for there was no German masterplan for a war against France and Britain as well as Poland. Hitler's invasion of Poland landed him with a conflict for which his armed forces were wholly unprepared. On the first day of World War II Karl Dönitz, commander of the still diminutive U-boat force, spelled out his position in a memorandum of admirable clarity:

'With 22 boats and a prospective increase of one to two boats a month I am incapable of undertaking efficacious measures against England.'

It only remained to be seen how prepared were the victors of 1918 to undertake efficacious measures against the U-boats.

Above: Airship 'Submarine Scout Zero' comes in to land on HMS *Furious* in 1918. Before the development of aircraft-carriers, these 'blimps' provided the first effective air patrols against U-boats. Below: German seaplanes attack British submarine *C25* off Harwich (6 July 1918). Bombs and machine-gun fire killed the British captain and five ratings, preventing *C25* from diving. Despite a second air attack she was eventually towed into port by another submarine (*E51*).

peacetime defence cuts and the lack of impetus. To the victorious Allied sea powers in 1919 it seemed enough to prohibit Germany from retaining or ever building submarines again. The League of Nations predictably denounced unrestricted submarine warfare as an outrage against civilisation, reaffirming the pre-1914 Hague Convention Prize Laws. This cannot be written off as wishful thinking in the light of previous experience, for there was similar wishful thinking behind the rebirth of a German U-boat force in the middle 1930s. When the German Navy began to rearm in the late 1920s it did so under the comforting assumption—confirmed by Chancellor Hitler's original assurances to Grand-Admiral Raeder in 1933—that Germany would never fight Britain again. By 1938–39, five years after the first 250-ton 'Type 2' U-boats had been laid down, it was a different story. The German naval 'Z Plan' of January 1939 aimed at building a balanced fleet—battleships, aircraft-carriers, cruisers, destroyers

# 3. 1939-1945

Previous pages: Victim of the usually unsung Battle of the Pacific, a sinking Japanese freighter, victim of the American submarine USS *Drum*. Below: Close-up of *U-38*'s conning-tower, her crew at attention as she passes Grand-Admiral Raeder in review after one of her first war patrols in October 1939. *U-38* and *U-37* were the only two of the eight Type IXA boats to survive the Battle of the Atlantic; both were scuttled in German waters on 5 May 1945.

The most enduring myth about Nazi Germany and the outbreak of World War II is the belief that in September 1939 Germany was armed to the teeth and all set for world conquest. In fact none of the German armed forces was ready for anything more ambitious than a 'one-off' campaign against Poland. The Luftwaffe had no heavy bombers. The Army had no heavy tanks and still relied on horse-drawn transport. And the Navy, which in the decade before 1914 had been built up deliberately for a showdown with Britain, had in September 1939 spent most of the prewar decade under the assumption that a second naval confrontation with Britain was out of the question. The construction of a submarine fleet capable of waging another killer offensive against British merchant shipping had scarcely begun, and the Navy's U-boats suffered the same fate as the Luftwaffe's bombers and the Army's tanks. To build up numbers quickly, the decision was made to concentrate production on the medium types already in production at the outset of the war.

Hitler's war strategy was strictly opportunist and he began by being as anxious as the Allies to contain and limit the war, sparing no effort to soothe the apprehension of neutrals. The latent unreality of this policy, under which the U-boats went to war ordered to observe the Prize Regulations, was demonstrated on the first day of the war. On 3 September *Kapitänleutnant* Julius Lemp, patrolling the Western Approaches in *U-30*, torpedoed and sank the British liner *Athenia*. He claimed that he had mistaken her for a troopship. The incident was

a propaganda boon to both sides, the Germans replying to British denunciations of the atrocity by asserting that *Athenia* had been sunk by the British to discredit Germany. In practical terms the incident induced the British and French to accelerate the institution of coastal and oceanic convoys.

When Britain and France declined to make peace after the defeat of Poland, restrictions on U-boat operations were progressively lifted from 23 September until, on 17 November, they were allowed to attack liners without warning 'if clearly identifiable as hostile'. Though there never was a formal German proclamation of unrestricted submarine warfare, as there had been in 1917, the latter had in fact come into being in the first two months of the war, preceded by its antidote: convoy. Here at least was one respect in which the lessons of World War I had been learned and applied within the opening months of World War II.

Down to the end of 1939 the U-boats' main prey was the host of unescorted merchantmen caught overseas by the outbreak of war and making lone runs for home. As these could not be given the protection of convoy, their losses, though high, would have been even higher if Dönitz had had more U-boats at sea. Between September and December 1939 114 British, Allied and neutral merchantmen fell victim to U-boats (421,156 tons in all), only four of them in convoy. These casualties were predictable. A far bigger worry by November and December 1939 was the rapidly mounting toll of sinkings in British coastal waters, caused by the first German 'secret weapon' to be unleashed in the war: the magnetic mine. Laid on the sea bed in shallow coastal waters, this weapon was detonated by a ship's magnetic field passing overhead and could not be swept by conventional means. In November and December 1939, when the U-boats accounted for only 47 merchantmen, 59 ships were sunk by mines. But when a magnetic mine was accidentally dropped on a tidal mud flat exposed at low water (23 November) the British were able to dismantle the weapon, discover its polarity and develop effective countermeasures. Without this piece of luck the magnetic mine (of which only about 1500 had been manufactured by the outbreak of war) could well have succeeded in paralysing convoy traffic between Britain's east coast ports and the Thames estuary.

For Dönitz and his U-boat captains, however, the biggest query in the opening weeks of the war was the effectiveness of the loudly pro-

claimed British device for locating submerged submarines. This was known as 'asdic', using the initials of the Anti-Submarine Detection Investigation Committee originally formed in 1917. Mounted beneath a ship's hull, asdic (or 'sonar', as it is known today and will be so termed in this book) sends a regular sonic pulse or 'ping' echoing through the water in a cone-shaped beam. This can be swung from side to side to enable a wider search to be made. When a submarine is found by the beam the 'ping' comes back with an echo which, unless the submarine gets clear of the beam like an aero-plane escaping from a searchlight, enables the hunter to track down the submarine and attack. The development of a workable sonar system in the second half of the 1930s was the vital break-through in undersea war; but the British Naval Staff was being wildly optimistic when it reported in 1937 that 'the submarine should never again be able to present us with the problem we were faced with in 1917'.

It was not yet appreciated that the effective-ness of sonar depended on trained operators who had developed an indefinable extra sense; a special 'ear' which told them at once when a 'contact' was a submarine and not a shoal of fish. It also depended on escort commanders able to 'out-think' the submarine skipper they were hunting, and on close, sometimes intuitive teamwork between escorts. Not all of this experience could be built up in peacetime exercises; it could only be fully attained at sea in wartime. Moreover, in September 1939 the fitting of sonar to every warship in the Royal Navy was only just getting under way.

The limited reach of early sonar made it no more than a tool enabling defensive escorts to counterattack, but the British began World War II by repeating their original mistake of the last war, and tried to use it offensively. They patrolled likely U-boat hunting-grounds with aircraft carriers escorted by destroyers fitted with sonar and this, as soon transpired, was a profligate risk. On 14 September *Ark Royal's* hunting group blundered across *U-39*, which fired four torpedoes at the carrier. Only the fact that the torpedoes' magnetic pistols detonated prematurely saved *Ark Royal* and betrayed *U-39's* presence to the destroyers, which closed in amid a flurry of depth-charge attacks. Too damaged to escape, *U-39* surfaced and her crew surrendered—the first U-boat lost in the war. But only three days later the U-boats got their revenge. On 17 September *Kapitänleutnant* Otto Schuhart in *U-29* was stalking a merchantman

in the St George's Channel when he sighted the carrier *Courageous*. He stalked his new prey for over two hours without being detected either by the escorts' sonar or the carrier's aircraft, then sank *Courageous* with three torpedoes. The escorting destroyers failed to locate *U-29*, which escaped, having given the British a salutary lesson that sonar still had its

Top: Type IIB U-boat. Above: An easy daylight kill on the surface. The U-boat has been trimmed down with only the upper casing awash, to ensure the torpedo an undisturbed run below the surface.

limitations. Aircraft carriers were promptly withdrawn from the anti-U-boat patrols.

Determined to gain the moral initiative, as the first U-boats had done at the outset of World War I, Dönitz planned an audacious coup: the penetration of Scapa Flow by a lone U-boat. After 20 years of increasing neglect and peacetime economies the Flow's defences were a pale ghost of what they had been in 1918. Dönitz, studying World War I experience and the latest air reconnaisance photographs, correctly de-

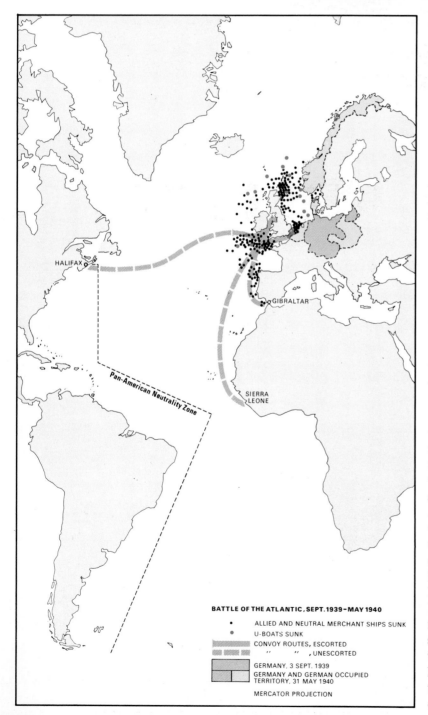

BATTLE OF THE ATLANTIC, SEPT. 1939-MAY 1940

- ALLIED AND NEUTRAL MERCHANT SHIPS SUNK
- U-BOATS SUNK
- CONVOY ROUTES, ESCORTED
- " " , UNESCORTED
- GERMANY, 3 SEPT. 1939
- GERMANY AND GERMAN OCCUPIED TERRITORY, 31 MAY 1940
- MERCATOR PROJECTION

duced that Kirk Sound, east of the Flow, had not been completely sealed with blockships. *Kapitänleutnant* Günther Prien and *U-47* undertook the mission, entered the Flow on the night of 13–14 October, and sank the old battleship *Royal Oak*. Luckily for the British she was the only capital ship there. It was a decided anticlimax for Prien, who disguised the fact in his report and delighted the German propaganda machine with a wonderful tale—how he pressed home his attack, exposed under a sky bright with Northern Lights, then escaped while the Flow sprang to life and hunting destroyers churned up the water with panicky depth-charge attacks. The *Royal Oak* affair was a distasteful and untypical example of a brave and resourceful submariner (Prien was an enthusiastic Nazi, unlike most of his comrades) playing the propagandists' game. Prien's exploit caused the withdrawal of the British Home Fleet from Scapa Flow until the defences could be restored. During the Fleet's absence the battleship *Nelson* and brand-new cruiser *Belfast* were badly damaged by mines.

By the end of March 1940 the balance in the U-boat war seemed, if anything, to be tilting in the Allies' favour. Nine U-boats had been sunk in 1939, six of them seagoing Type VIIs suitable for Atlantic cruises. Another five Type VIIs were sunk between January and March 1940, and two of the newer, faster Type IXs. But after April 1940 the balance swung decisively in the Germans' favour. They isolated and corrected the torpedo fault (causing premature explosions or no explosions at all) which plagued the U-boats operating in northern latitudes during the Norwegian campaign (8 April–8 June). On 5 May the British submarine *Seal*, disabled by a mine, was captured in the Kattegat by German seaplanes. She was found to have steel torpedo tubes—a revelation to German designers, who had always taken it for granted that torpedo tubes had to be cast from bronze. The adoption of steel tubes in preference to bronze removed

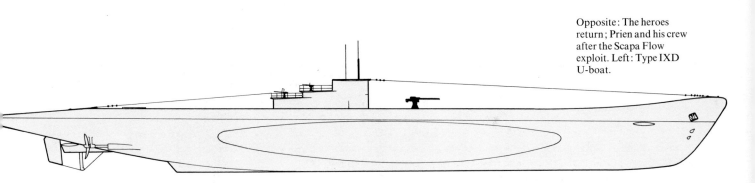

Opposite: The heroes
return; Prien and his crew
after the Scapa Flow
exploit. Left: Type IXD
U-boat.

one of the tightest bottlenecks from the U-boat
construction programme. But nothing compared
to the strategic advantage won by the German
land victories between 10 May and 25 June
1940: the conquests not only of Norway but of
Holland, Belgium and France. On 7 July *U-30*
became the first U-boat to use the Biscay port of
Lorient as a supply base, and in late August,
before the air battle of Britain had reached its
climax, Dönitz moved his operational headquarters from Wilhelmshaven to Lorient.

By the beginning of September 1940 the
fortunes of war had so perfectly balanced U-
boat losses and new construction that Dönitz
had precisely the same number of U-boats as on
the first day of the war: 57. The vital difference
was that the seagoing Type VIIs and IXs could
now be based on the Biscay coast instead of
having to make the long outward voyage round
the British Isles to reach the Western Approaches. Dönitz could therefore sail enough
U-boats at a time to confront every Atlantic
convoy to Britain with sustained group attacks
by half a dozen U-boats or more. This was the
*rudeltaktik* or 'pack tactics' with which he
himself had experimented in 1918, and in which
he had trained his U-boat commanders. The era
of the 'wolf-packs' had began.

*Rudeltaktik* was simple and flexible. A single
U-boat sighting a convoy would tag along,
reporting the convoy's size, position and course
to Dönitz's headquarters. All U-boats with a
chance of intercepting would then be homed on
to the convoy. The actual attacks were made
on the surface at night. First and foremost, this
exploited the simple fact that a submarine's
conning-tower is virtually impossible to spot at
night, whereas the bulky silhouette of even a
blacked-out merchantman stands out against
the sky. Second, it rendered the escort's sonar
useless, for sonar could not detect *surfaced*
submarines. Third, a U-boat running on diesels
had the speed with which to keep pace with the
convoy, attacking, breaking off and returning

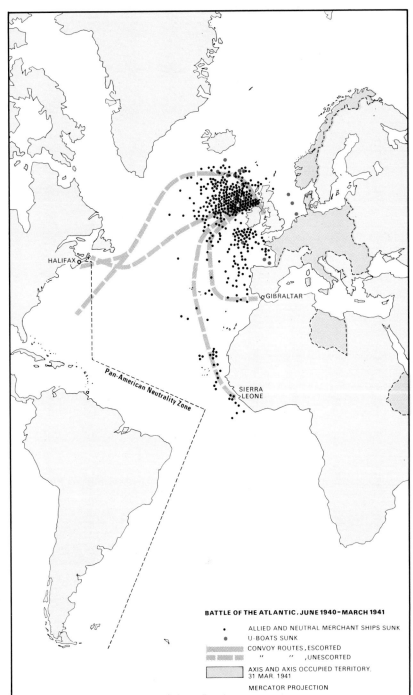

BATTLE OF THE ATLANTIC, JUNE 1940-MARCH 1941

. ALLIED AND NEUTRAL MERCHANT SHIPS SUNK

• U-BOATS SUNK

CONVOY ROUTES, ESCORTED

" " ,UNESCORTED

AXIS AND AXIS OCCUPIED TERRITORY,
31 MAR. 1941

MERCATOR PROJECTION

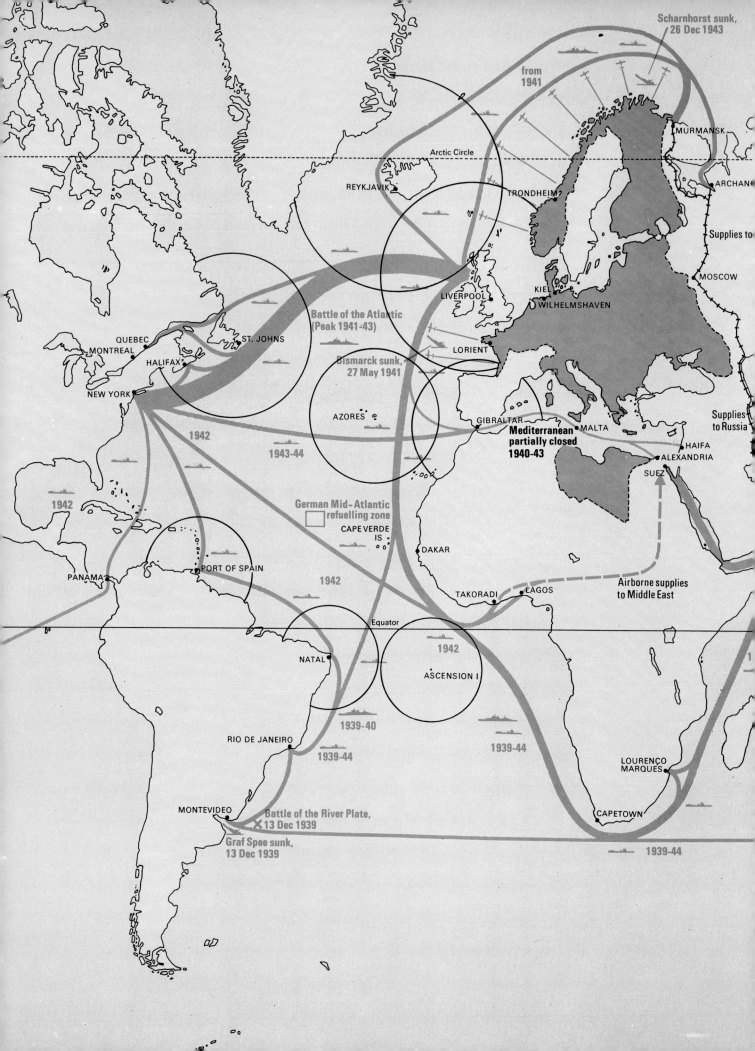

Scharnhorst sunk,
26 Dec 1943

MURMANSK

ARCHAN

Arctic Circle

from
1941

Supplies to

REYKJAVIK

TRONDHEIM

MOSCOW

KIEL

WILHELMSHAVEN

LIVERPOOL

Battle of the Atlantic
(Peak 1941-43)

LORIENT

QUEBEC

MONTREAL

ST. JOHNS

HALIFAX

Bismarck sunk,
27 May 1941

GIBRALTAR

MALTA

Supplies
to Russia

NEW YORK

Mediterranean
partially closed
1940-43

HAIFA

AZORES

ALEXANDRIA

SUEZ

1942

1943-44

German Mid-Atlantic
refuelling zone

CAPE VERDE
IS

1942

DAKAR

Airborne supplies
to Middle East

PANAMA

PORT OF SPAIN

TAKORADI

LAGOS

1942

Equator

1942

NATAL

ASCENSION I

1939-40

RIO DE JANEIRO

1939-44

1939-44

LOURENÇO
MARQUES

MONTEVIDEO

Battle of the River Plate,
13 Dec 1939

CAPETOWN

Graf Spee sunk,
13 Dec 1939

1939-44

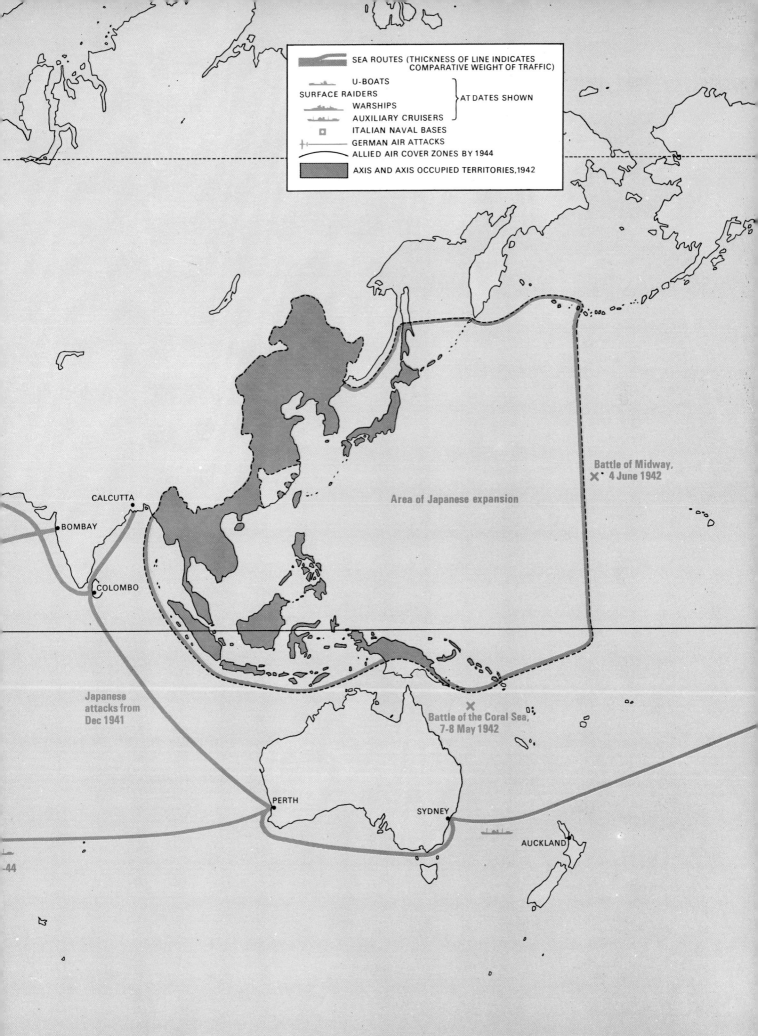

SEA ROUTES (THICKNESS OF LINE INDICATES
COMPARATIVE WEIGHT OF TRAFFIC)

U-BOATS
SURFACE RAIDERS
WARSHIPS
AUXILIARY CRUISERS
ITALIAN NAVAL BASES
GERMAN AIR ATTACKS
ALLIED AIR COVER ZONES BY 1944

AXIS AND AXIS OCCUPIED TERRITORIES, 1942

AT DATES SHOWN

CALCUTTA

BOMBAY

COLOMBO

Area of Japanese expansion

Battle of Midway,
4 June 1942

Japanese
attacks from
Dec 1941

Battle of the Coral Sea,
7-8 May 1942

PERTH

SYDNEY

AUCKLAND

-44

MERCATOR PROJECTION

to the attack. A surfaced U-boat could usually outpace anything but a destroyer, and even against a pursuing destroyer a U-boat had a tighter turning circle. Fourth, surfaced action at night enabled the U-boats to keep radio contact with their headquarters, as they could only use their radio when surfaced.

When the new attacks began in September–October 1940 the U-boats had yet another advantage. Peacetime parsimony, the belated reappearance of a German submarine force, and over-confidence in the powers of sonar had left the Royal Navy starved of small warships suited for work as Atlantic convoy escorts. Until the threat of a German invasion receded in October, every available British destroyer was kept in home waters for action against the expected invasion fleet. Thus fast convoys bound for Britain from Halifax (HX) and slow convoys from Sydney, Cape Breton (SC) would sail perhaps with an escort consisting of a single sloop, or armed merchant cruiser. On reaching the meridian of 15° West (the north-south line about 50 miles west of Rockall) HX and SC convoys would be met by escorts from the out-ward-bound convoys, which were dispersed at this handover point. The resultant scatter of dispersed shipping, stragglers and incoming convoys which had not yet picked up their escorts provided a wolves' banquet for the U-boats—the first 'happy time', as German submariners called it. The British were rushing through an emergency escort-building pro-gramme, and begged 50 ancient destroyers from the United States (all of which had to be fitted with sonar before they were of any use against the U-boats). But until these stop-gap escorts joined the battle and reached full combat efficiency the U-boats had things all their own

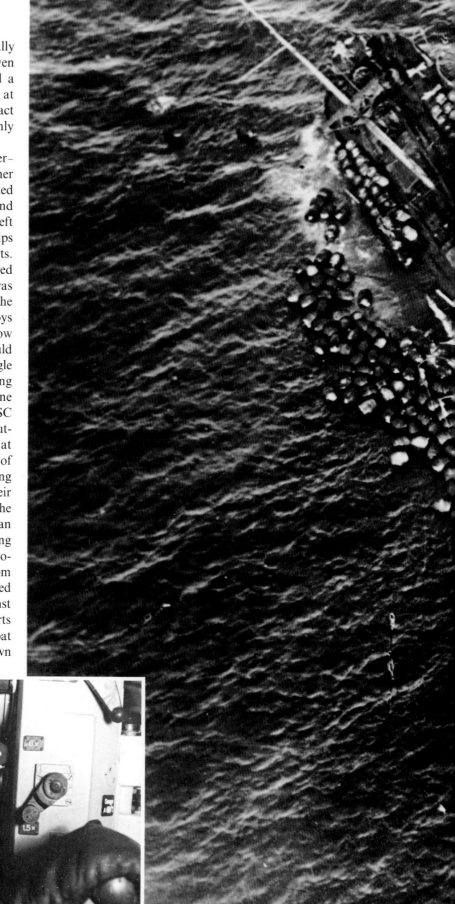

U-boat commander at the periscope (set to low magnification).

Death-throes of a merchantman, rolling helplessly to starboard and spilling her deck cargo of barrels into the sea.

Type VIIb U-boat

way. In October 1940 they sank 63 British, Allied and neutral merchantmen (352,407 tons), 56 of them in the North Atlantic.

Of the many isolated factors which helped save Britain in 1940, three were of particular importance. The first was the unexpected bonus of nearly four million tons of Norwegian, Dutch, Belgian and French merchant shipping which sought refuge in Britain after the German conquest of western Europe. The second was the natural failure of the U-boats to concentrate all their efforts on shipping bound for Britain. They went for the easy meat, the stragglers and dispersed ships, mainly outward bound. These sinkings were no less dangerous to Britain in the long term, but they allowed enough homeward-bound shipping to arrive for Britain to hold on until the foul weather of the winter months caused a fall-off in losses. And the third factor was the uncurbed arrogance and incompetence of *Reichsmarschall* Hermann Göring, overlord of the Luftwaffe, to whom the British really ought to put up a statue. Having failed to prevent the British Army from escaping at Dunkirk, then thrown away victory over RAF Fighter Command in the Battle of Britain, Göring refused to co-operate with the German Navy and release the aircraft needed to set up a German 'fleet air arm'. Insisting that 'everything that flies belongs to me', Göring also refused to place all available long-range reconnaissance and bomber aircraft, particularly suited to scouting over the eastern Atlantic, at the Navy's disposal.

Though starved of the invaluable airborne intelligence which they could have used, the U-boat commanders in October put up a performance which they were never to equal: an average *daily* total of 920 tons sunk. One of their biggest successes was the assault on SC-7 and HX-79 (16–20 October), when six U-boats sank

32 merchantmen and damaged four others. SC-7 lost 58.8 percent sunk and damaged, HX-79 24.5 percent, and the only reason their losses were not higher was the fact that the U-boats ran out of torpedoes. On the British side this double battle was marked by a complete failure to come to grips with the U-boats, despite the apparent strength of the escort (two destroyers, four corvettes, three trawlers and a minesweeper) which met HX-79.

Type VIIc U-boat:
Length 220 feet
Breadth 20 feet
Draught 15¾ feet
Surface displacement 769 tons
Maximum speed surfaced 17 knots
Maximum speed submerged 7.6 knots

Endurance surfaced 6,500 miles
Endurance submerged 80 miles
Armament: 5 × 21 inch torpedo tubes, 14 torpedoes

1 × 88mm gun, 1 × 20mm machine gun (after 1943 replaced by 1 × 37mm Flak) 2 twin 20mm Flak machine guns

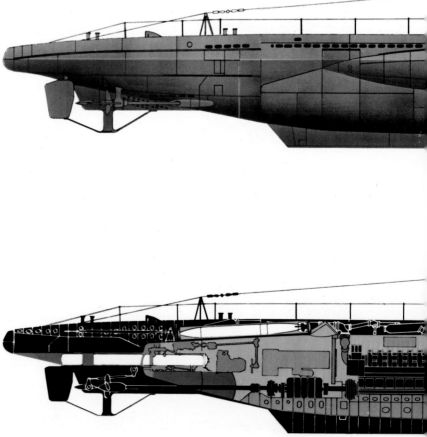

Above left : British
submarines alongside their
tender. Above : U-boat
crewmen on watch in the
Atlantic.

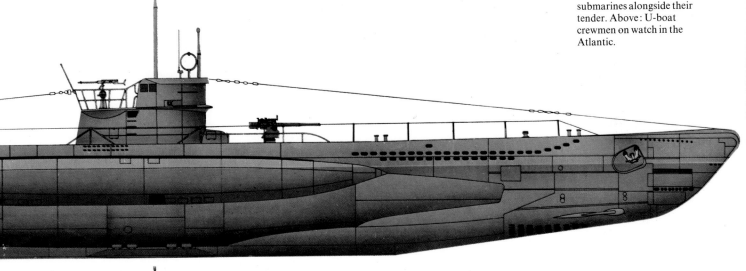

In these early days, the British attempts at offensive-defensive tactics played right into the U-boat commanders' hands. Escorts tended to charge off in pursuit of a contact or reported periscope sighting and spend far too much time on these wild-goose chases before rejoining their charges. Meanwhile the U-boats worked in close to the convoy and set about their work, virtually uninterrupted. It was at this time that 'Silent Otto' Kretschmer of *U-99* perfected his technique of working his way *inside* the convoy,

between the columns of merchantmen. He went on to become the top-scoring U-boat ace of World War II, with a total of 44 merchantmen (266,629 tons) and one destroyer sunk. He and his comrades certainly had all the scope they needed. In the case of SC-7 the British only had two sloops and a single corvette with which to defend 30 merchant ships taking up five square miles of ocean.

The following table shows the peaks of success reached by the U-boats during the Battle of the Atlantic after their devastating beginning in October 1940:

| Month/ Year | Merchant ships sunk (tons) | U-boats operational | U-boats sunk |
|---|---|---|---|
| October 1940 | 63 (352,407) | 27 | 1 |
| June 1941 | 61 (310,143) | 65 | 4 |
| June 1942 | 124 (623,545) | 140 | 3 |
| March 1943 | 82 (476,349) | 240 | 15 |

From a strategic viewpoint the Battle fell into three phases. The first (August 1940–December 1941) saw the U-boats easily take the strain as the Royal Navy's escort famine began to ease at last, and as escort commanders began to apply more successful tactics. The second phase (December 1941–June 1942) saw the entry into the war of the United States (a country almost totally unprepared for undersea war) bring little or no immediate easement on the Atlantic convoy routes. This was the second 'happy time', as the U-boats again went for the easy meat—this time along the American seaboard. The third phase (June 1942–May 1943) saw the U-boats, now over five times more numerous than in October 1940, going all-out for the domination of the North Atlantic—only to fail spectacularly, with unprecedented loss. And their failure lay in the growing inability of the U-boats to wage commerce warfare against a formidable combination of new technology, new weaponry and new tactics painfully developed over the past three years.

By the spring of 1941 the most urgent requirement of the British—more escorts—was being fulfilled as the stop-gap vessels ordered in 1939 and 1940 continued to be rushed into service. Their original requirement was simple: to be able to operate in the North Atlantic, carrying sonar and depth-charges. But from March 1941

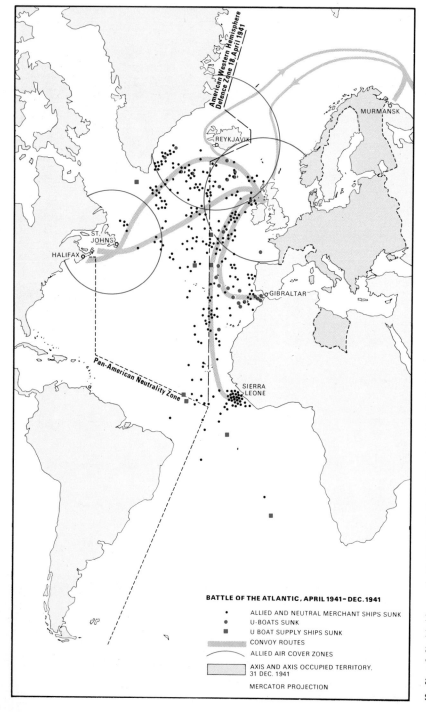

BATTLE OF THE ATLANTIC, APRIL 1941–DEC. 1941

· ALLIED AND NEUTRAL MERCHANT SHIPS SUNK
● U-BOATS SUNK
■ U BOAT SUPPLY SHIPS SUNK
CONVOY ROUTES
ALLIED AIR COVER ZONES
AXIS AND AXIS OCCUPIED TERRITORY, 31 DEC. 1941
MERCATOR PROJECTION

they began to carry additional equipment which, when tested and proven, added significantly to their effectiveness. First came the newly developed 10cm Type 271 radar, whose narrow beam could locate a U-boat's conning tower (and, given ideal conditions, a periscope) even on a pitch-dark night. Then came High Frequency Direction Finding—HF/DF or 'Huff-Duff', which latched on to U-boat radio messages and enabled a U-boat's position to be plotted with lightning speed, no matter how short the intercepted message might be. Like Type 271 radar, 'Huff-Duff' was a standard fitting in new escort vessels by the end of 1941.

The invaluable British lead in radar development provided the next important weapon for fighting the U-boats: ASV (Air/Surface Vessel) radar, suitable for fitting in long-range shore-based patrol aircraft. As its name implies it could locate surfaced submarines as well as ordinary ships, but its weakness was that the radar contact tended to fade at short range as the aircraft came in at low level to attack. The answer to this particular problem was the 'Leigh Light', an intensely bright narrow-beam search-light carried by the aircraft, used to illuminate the target once the ASV radar indicated that the target should be within visual range. By the summer of 1942 ASV radar and the Leigh Light were making surface runs in the Bay of Biscay suicidal for U-boats leaving or returning to port. The U-boat, roaring along on its diesels, would suddenly be dazzled by the Leigh Light's beam after the attacking aircraft had followed up an ASV contact with a stealthy approach. This the Germans countered, for a time success-

fully (July 1942–March 1943), with the Metox radar detector, known as the 'Biscay Cross' from its simple cruciform aerial. Metox told the U-boat when it was under radar surveillance and provided an eight-month respite from ASV and Leigh Light detection until the crucial month of March 1943, when the first successful contact was made with 10cm ASV which Metox could not detect.

Unless the U-boat was damaged or determined to fight it out on the surface, an aircraft pouncing on a surfaced U-boat normally only had a matter of seconds in which to attack before the U-boat dived. Once the U-boat was down it could change course sharply and make off while the aircraft depth-charged the area where the U-boat had last been seen. Once air-to-surface engagements became commonplace the British were able to analyse the problem and see that normal depth-charge settings were no use; the U-boat had no time to get down to the depth at which the charges were set to detonate. The answer to this was a new choice of shallow-depth settings from as little as 25 feet, which

Above: This U-boat is either unable to dive or has chosen to fight it out on the surface. Her diesels are clearly still delivering full power but the attacking Sunderland's last pattern of depth charges has straddled her amidships, ensuring her doom. Left: The deadly eye—Leigh Light on a Sunderland, for pinpointing surfaced U-boats at night.

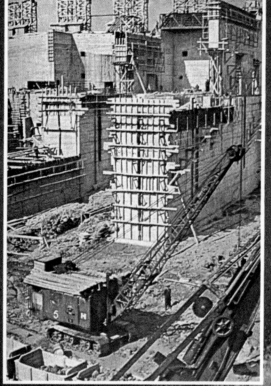

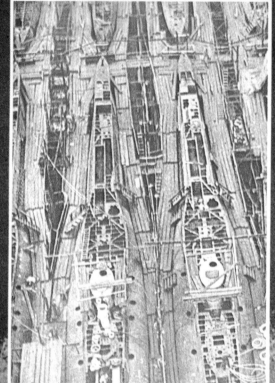

Far left: Building U-boat
pens, bomb-proof until the
RAF adopted the
devastating 'Tallboy' bomb.
Left: U-boats in mass
production. Right: A
U-boat's ensign, the Reich
'War Banner'. Far right: A
tanker burns. Below: British
destroyer men hungrily
await the results of a depth-
charge attack.

Opposite: Aerial view of an escort's attack, with an encouraging oil slick welling from the turmoil of her last depth-charge. Opposite below: Depth-charge on its thrower. Right: 'Hedgehog' grenades mounted for firing (below) and (top) hitting the water.

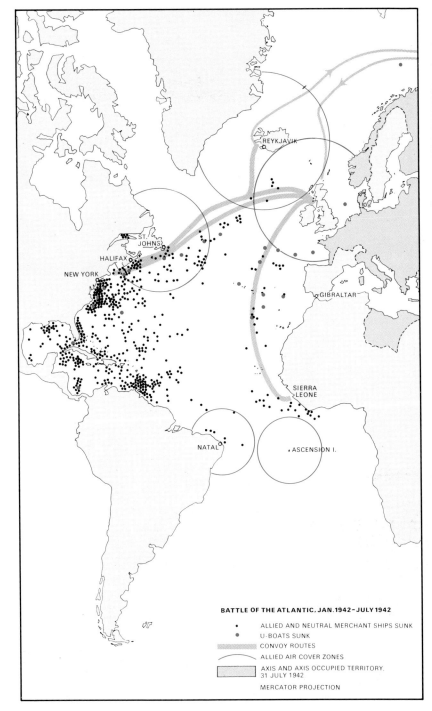

BATTLE OF THE ATLANTIC, JAN.1942 – JULY 1942

- ALLIED AND NEUTRAL MERCHANT SHIPS SUNK
- U-BOATS SUNK
- CONVOY ROUTES
- ALLIED AIR COVER ZONES
- AXIS AND AXIS OCCUPIED TERRITORY, 31 JULY 1942

MERCATOR PROJECTION

caught the U-boat when it was still close to the surface and pushed up the rate of sinkings by air attack fourfold.

To make certain of a U-boat, however, surface escorts had to try and pass directly overhead, 'running down' the sonar contact until the accelerating echo return formed an uninterrupted tone. Against an experienced U-boat commander, wise in judging escorts' behaviour by hydrophone, this was hard to achieve. Escort commanders clamoured for a weapon which could be hurled ahead of an escort running down a contact. The result was the 'Hedgehog' projector which threw 24 small bombs, fused to explode on contact, over a range of 250 yards. 'Hedgehog's' great advantage was that it gave the U-boat on the receiving end no advance warning to take evasive action, which conventional depth-charge attacks did. 'Hedgehog' came into service early in 1943, in time for the crisis of the Atlantic battle. Other unwelcome surprises for the U-boats at this time were the new deep setting of 500 feet for depth-charges and the technique of enabling escorts to fire much denser patterns of ten charges. These, like 'Hedgehog' exploited the scatter effect and increased the chances of a hit.

Tactics improved rapidly after the establishment of a tactical evaluation and training school by Captain Gilbert Roberts in January 1942 — the first time that the hard-won experience of

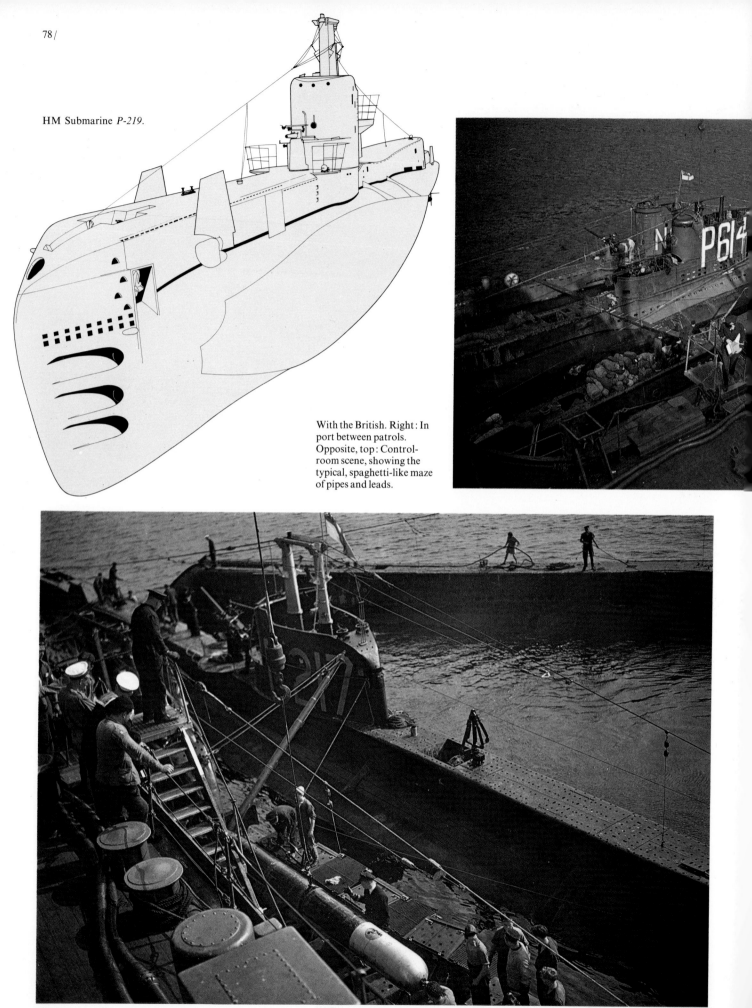

HM Submarine *P-219*.

With the British. Right: In port between patrols. Opposite, top: Control-room scene, showing the typical, spaghetti-like maze of pipes and leads.

The British take charge of a new 'fish'.

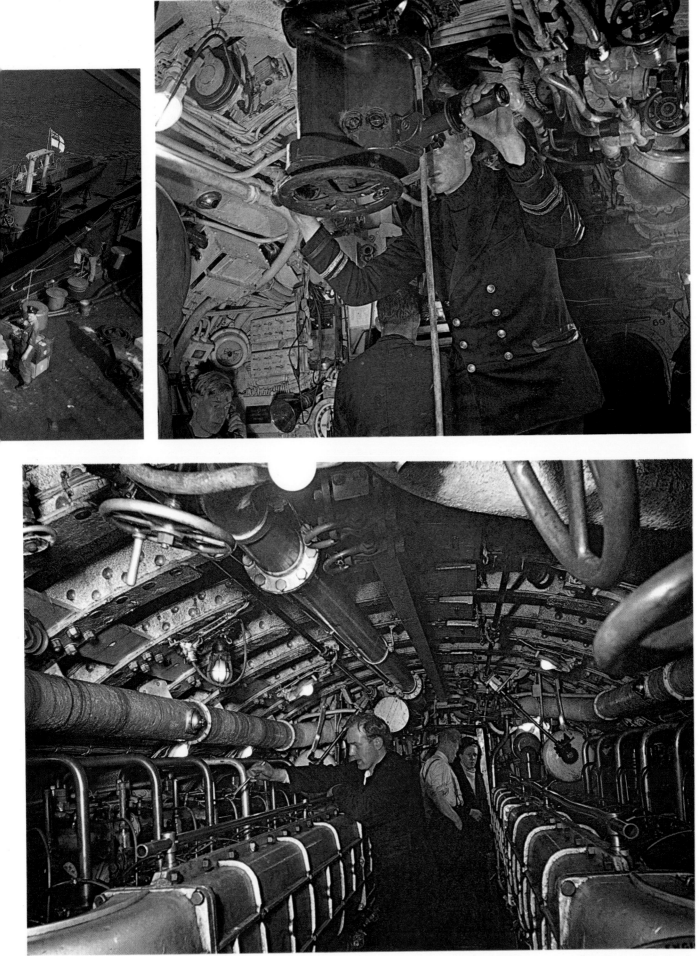

The British engine-room crew amid the roar of the diesels.

escort commanders was used to established how the U-boats were operating, and how best the escorts could collaborate in defence. In this collaboration a great boon was the American radio telephone, the TBS or 'talk between ships', cutting out the laborious signalling which did so much to slow down the escorts' reactions. With TBS and the new weaponry, the special escort groups, commanded by such veteran U-boat killers as Captain John Walker, Commander Peter Gretton and Captain Donald Macintyre, struck back with devastating effect in April and May 1943.

Even with all these new factors the final U-boat assault could hardly have been met without two other vital links in the Allied chain of survival. The first of these was the immense swelling of Allied merchant tonnage replacement by the American shipbuilding industry—a life-saving transfusion which, in early 1943, outstripped the losses to U-boats for the first time since autumn 1940. In July 1943, for the first time in the war, new tonnage overtook losses from *all* causes—submarines, mines, air and surface attack, collisions, weather and unknown causes combined. And the final link was the timely provision of long-range air cover over the 'Black Gap' in mid-Atlantic—the killing-ground, so long out of reach of shore-based aircraft, where the U-boats concentrated their last assault on the Allied Atlantic lifeline. The key air weapons were land-based B-24 Liberator bombers, and lightweight escort carriers to accompany the convoys. For the past six months the escort carriers and support groups had been drawn away from the Atlantic to cover the convoys first carrying, then supplying the Allied invasion of northwest Africa—Operation Torch. When the escort carriers and support groups were released and rushed back to the North Atlantic at the end of March 1943, they came in the nick of time. Out of a total of 240 operational U-boats, Dönitz had committed no less than 112 to severing the Atlantic convoy route.

Such an unprecedented concentration—which was only ever reached in the North Atlantic—

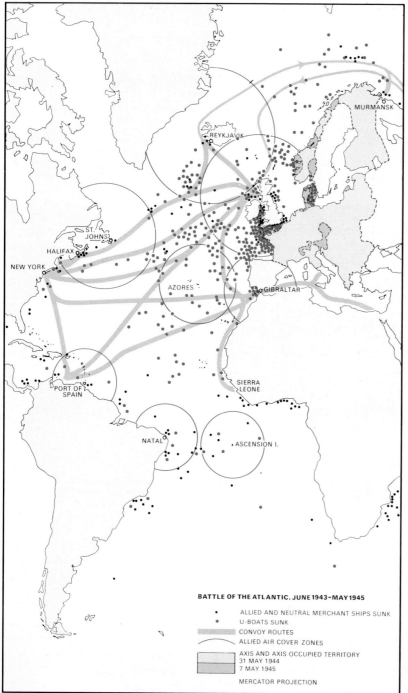

BATTLE OF THE ATLANTIC, JUNE 1943–MAY 1945

- • ALLIED AND NEUTRAL MERCHANT SHIPS SUNK
- • U-BOATS SUNK
- CONVOY ROUTES
- ALLIED AIR COVER ZONES
- AXIS AND AXIS OCCUPIED TERRITORY
  31 MAY 1944
  7 MAY 1945

MERCATOR PROJECTION

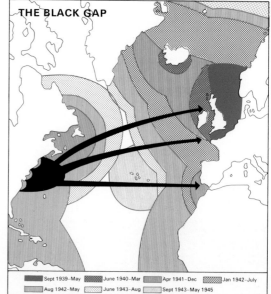

THE BLACK GAP

| Sept 1939–May | June 1940–Mar | Apr 1941–Dec | Jan 1942–July |
| Aug 1942–May | June 1943–Aug | Sept 1943–May 1945 |

The prefabricated, mass-produced 'Liberty Ship', potent weapon in the Atlantic battle. Top: A typical cargo. Above: Hoisting aboard a prefabricated deckhouse section. Right: Liberty Ships in varying stages of completion at the Kaiser yards in 1943. The ship in the centre is about to be launched.

proved capable of overwhelming conventional escort forces lacking hunter-killer support groups, long-range air patrols and escort carriers. Before these returned to the North Atlantic at the end of March 1943, the escorts of convoys SC-122 and HX-229 were swamped by a concentration of 38 U-boats as the two convoys struggled across the 'Black Gap' (15–19 March). Out of 92 ships, 21 (141,000 tons) were sunk for the loss of only one U-boat. But the passage of ONS-5 (22 April–6 May) was a very different story. Thirty U-boats were concentrated against this convoy of 40 (the latter considerably disrupted by atrocious weather) and managed to sink 21 merchant ships—but it cost them no less than seven U-boats.

With one U-boat being sunk for every three merchant ships, small wonder that the still-dense U-boat packs showed increasing reluctance to press home attacks on succeeding convoys, though well-placed to do so. In the decisive convoy battles of May a staggering total of 41 U-boats was sunk: 14 by surface escorts, 11 by air escorts, the rest on passage. Losses on this scale threatened nothing but the early annihilation of the entire U-boat force. In 1942 87 U-boats had been sunk, an average of 7.25 per month, bringing the overall total of boats sunk since the outbreak of war to 153, or an average of 3.8 per month. But 96 U-boats were sunk in the period January–May 1943, pushing the average monthly losses up to 19.2 for that year and to

U-boat under attack from American carrier-based aircraft, summer 1943.

5.5 since the outbreak of war. Accepting the inevitable, Dönitz ordered his U-boats to withdraw from the North Atlantic routes on 24 May 1943.

The defeat of the U-boats in May 1943 was the defeat of the diesel-electric submarine by a combination which the Allies only managed to bring together at the last possible moment—carrier-based and long-range shore-based air cover, plus hunter-killer escort groups, HF/DF, 10cm radar and improved anti-submarine weapons and tactics. If Dönitz had had his 240 operational boats as late as 1942, long before all these improvements had been made to the defences and the transformed Allied shipbuilding programme had got under way, the Atlantic convoy route would most definitely have been severed and Britain probably starved into surrender by the end of the year.

But one of the main reasons for Germany losing World War II was the built-in opportunism of German grand strategy, with the resultant failure to concentrate on the Allies' weakest points. Dönitz's pleas to be allowed to concentrate his efforts in the North Atlantic were overruled after Rommel's first offensive opened a promising new front in North Africa (March–April 1941). Dönitz was subsequently ordered to divert U-boats to the Mediterranean, and

American sailors take charge of their prey. *U-505*, surrendered off the Cape Verdes in June 1944.

also to the Far North to operate against the Allied convoys to Russia. The resultant dispersal of effort, which saw a grand total of 62 U-boats written off in the Mediterranean alone by the end of the war, was of vital importance to the Battle of the Atlantic. By the spring of 1942, far from preparing for a knock-out blow against the North Atlantic convoy route, the U-boat force was being diluted into no less than three sideshows: the Mediterranean, the Far North, and the easy killings off the American coast. This strategic blunder, for which Hitler and Grand-Admiral Raeder must share the blame, gave the Allies just enough margin in the North Atlantic on which to survive in 1942.

In the Mediterranean, British submarine operations against the Axis convoys carrying supplies to the German and Italian Armies in Africa were no less deadly than the efforts of the U-boats in the Atlantic, though on a smaller scale. The British attacks on the Axis Libyan convoy route were supplemented by air strikes from Malta, and the submarine flotilla based on the island gave the British submarine service its most famous aces of the war: Malcolm Wanklyn of *Upholder*, 'Tommo' Tomkinson of *Urge*, Alistair Mars of *Unbroken* and Ben Bryant of *Safari*. This 'front' of the undersea war was not, as in the North Atlantic, a matter of group attacks directed from a shore-based headquarters, but of individual flair on patrol. British submarine commanders were considerably helped by the Germans' and Italians' lack of the sophisticated detection equipment used against the U-boats in the Atlantic. They also had plenty of scope for the ideal use of the diesel-electric submarine, perfected by Lothar de la Perière and *U-35* in World War I: surface attack with the gun. During the air siege of Malta (January–May 1942) the submarines performed invaluable service as supply ships, a role to which they were hardly suited. Though forced to quit Malta for three months during the massive German air raids of April–early May 1942, the submarines returned in July, after Rommel had been finally halted at Alamein. From then on, again working in harness with the air strike forces, the Malta submarines kept Rommel starved of fuel and reinforcements until Montgomery attacked with crushing superiority in late October.

The negligible contribution of Italy's submarines to the undersea war was one of the most welcome surprises to the British. Italy came into the war in June 1940 with 100 submarines, double the German strength, but soon proved that mere numbers were of little use without aggressive and skilled commanders working to a prearranged tactical programme. Italy's submarines achieved nothing of any significance, either in commerce destruction or in operations against Allied warships. The 26 Italian submarines operating in the Atlantic by the end of 1940 failed ignominiously to share in the 'happy time' then being experienced by their German allies. In 1940 and 1941 the complete inability of the Italian submarines to impede, let alone cripple the British Mediterranean Fleet was a key motive for the diversion of German U-boats from the Atlantic to the Mediterranean. All the severe British naval losses to submarines in the

Mediterranean—the battleship *Barham*, air-craft-carriers *Eagle* and *Ark Royal*, the cruiser *Galatea*—were inflicted by German U-boats. By the time of the Italian surrender in September 1943, 86 Italian submarines had been sunk or captured—18 of them by British submarines—double the number of German U-boats sunk by Allied submarines since the outbreak of war.

By the second half of 1943 Dönitz and the U-boat designers were struggling to find an answer to the new air/sea superiority of the Allied escort forces. The German efforts to beat the escorts led to a host of experimental fittings, modifications, techniques and tactics. Some of these were fundamentally mistaken; others became essentials of postwar submarine design. Dönitz's initial order for U-boats to 'fight it out' with aircraft on the surface was a disastrous miscalculation; only a handful of Allied aircraft was actually shot down, and aircraft were always easier to replace than U-boats. Even when the latter were given 37mm and quadruple

Above: The shattering end of the British battleship *Barham*. Below: The last hours of *Ark Royal*, which went down as rescuers struggled to tow her into Gibraltar.

Top: Type XXI U-boat.
Above: Unfinished Type
XXIs pack the slipways at
Hamburg. Thanks to pre-
fabrication and the dispersal
of manufacture, Dönitz's
fleet of Type XXIs was
fast nearing completion by
the spring of 1945.

20mm AA guns the odds remained in the attackers' favour, and between June and December 1943 95 U-boats were sunk by aircraft alone.

Against the surface escorts the Germans adopted the *Zaunkönig* acoustic torpedo, which homed on high-speed engine noises. Though this primitive homing torpedo obliged Allied escorts to stream noise-emitting 'Foxers' it could not, once the mass attacks on the convoys had been suspended, reverse the course of the Atlantic battle by itself. Less successful was the *bold* or *pillenwerfer*, akin to the decoy cloud of ink emitted by a panicked octopus or squid. The *bold* was a slug of chemicals which, on ejection from the U-boat, foamed into a dense cloud of bubbles capable of returning a sonar echo. Trained sonar operators, however, soon learned to tell the difference. Nor could either the sharp ear of sonar nor radar be foiled by the expedient of covering U-boats with absorbent rubber (*sumpf*). But when the Germans turned

to the *schnorkel* as yet another possible answer to their troubles in the undersea war, they opened a radical new chapter in the history of submarine development.

The *schnorkel* was not originally a German device; it was developed before the war by the Dutch, and fell into German hands when Holland capitulated in 1940. It enabled a submarine to run on diesels, either trimmed down or at periscope depth, with only a small air-breathing and exhaust head showing above the surface. Originally a device for stretching the life of a submarine's battery, the *schnorkel* offered the Germans a chance of preventing their U-boats being detected by radar and Leigh Light while recharging their batteries on the surface. Small though it was, a *schnorkel* head was not 'radar-proof', but when fitted with a radar detection device it gave prompt notice of Allied surveillance. And though a 'schnorkelling' U-boat had to keep its speed down to about six knots it had a vastly improved range over a boat forced to rely on its electric engine for maybe 20 hours out of the 24. When there was enough surface wind to dispel the cloud of exhaust smoke, a *schnorkel* was hard to spot from the air. It was easily confused with breaking waves, 'willywaws' or miniature waterspouts travelling along the surface, and even spouting whales. In the last nine months of the war Coastal Command aircraft 'sighted' 216 *schnorkels* in British home waters, only 88 of which (from the number of U-boats actually at sea) can have been genuine sightings.

To the old U-boats with which Dönitz had fought and lost the first round of the Battle of the Atlantic, the *schnorkel* was of little practical use as a potential war-winner. But when fitted to the new, high-speed boats rushed through production in the last 18 months of the war it created an entirely new weapons-system: the fast, long-range *true submarine*, as opposed to the *submersible* tied to the surface. The most revolutionary prototype was the Type XVIII, with its Walter turbine powered by 'Perhydrol': peroxide based, burned with oil, independent of outside ventilation and capable of delivering bursts of speed up to 25 knots. The biggest snag with the Walter turbine was the corrosive and highly explosive nature of the fuel—but this did not prevent a rushed development which only

helped further clog the already congested U-boat production pipeline. Far more promising was the Type XXI. Here was the ocean-going diesel/electric submarine rendered capable of all-submerged operations, using an improved *schnorkel* and silent 'creeping' electric motors. Another 'first' for the Type XXI was mechanised loading for the torpedoes, cutting out the need for boats to retire after the first attack in order to reload tubes.

With type XXIs Dönitz planned to reopen the Atlantic battle in 1945, using aggressive new tactics. The Type XXIs would use their speed to evade hunter-killer groups during approach, then get right *under* the convoys and riddle the merchantmen with acoustic torpedoes. Luckily for the Allies, 'peace' intervened—but one Type XXI captain, *Korvettenkapitän* Schnee, made a dummy attack on a British force on the eve of the surrender. Schnee rejoiced at the ease with which he went clean through the destroyer screen without being detected, then closed to an easy firing position on the cruiser in the centre. He then retired—again without being detected. But this demonstration of the Type XXI's potential took place on 30 April 1945—the day Hitler shot himself. Had the Type XXIs and their coastal counterparts, the Type XXIIIs, been ready a year earlier, they would certainly have been able to disrupt the Allied build-up for the invasion of Europe. Like the *Luftwaffe*'s Me262 jet fighter, which came too late to reverse the course of the war in the air, the Type XXI had fallen victim to the retention of obsolete types which had outlived their tactical usefulness.

It is only in comparatively recent years that attention has been given to the no less decisive 'Battle of the Pacific', which was the Atlantic ordeal turned inside out. In the Atlantic the Allies were on the defensive, trying to save

Left: Crew of a Japanese *Koryu* five-man boat. Below: Japanese submarine *I-2*. Bottom: Japanese Type *RO-7*.

Left and below: The end of the US carrier *Yorktown* in the Battle of Midway, June 1942. Badly damaged by Japanese carrier aircraft (left), *Yorktown* was finished off by the Japanese submarine *I-168*.

their sealanes from the assault of the U-boats. In the Pacific, however, the Japanese, having conquered Southeast Asia, the East Indies, and the islands of the west Pacific by autumn 1942, suffered a similar assault from American submarines and failed completely to mount an effective defence.

As far as submarine strategy was concerned the Japanese had not advanced since the end of World War I, when the current obsession had been to make submarines work with the battle fleets. In the first year of the Pacific War, from Pearl Harbor to Guadalcanal, Japanese submarines did well enough in this role, their most prestigious 'kills' being the American carriers *Yorktown* and *Wasp*. But by the end of 1942 the runaway sequence of Japanese victories had been stopped for good, and the outcome of the Pacific War was being decided in the battle of attrition on Guadalcanal in the Solomon Islands. To hold Guadalcanal, and all their other wide-spread conquests, the Japanese should have concentrated on severing the vital Allied supply link between the American west coast and Australia. Their failure even to attempt this strategy enabled the Americans first to take

Guadalcanal, then begin an advance up the Solomons chain in 1943.

Now the question was whether or not the Japanese Navy could defend the long sea routes connecting their far-flung island garrisons, and for this they were supremely ill-equipped. Their naval grand strategy was confined to

decisive operations with the 'Combined Fleet' of carrier strike forces and battle squadrons, and included no effective measures for the defence of the Japanese merchant navy. In December 1941, escort vessels ranked fifth in the Japanese naval building programme—a stark contrast to the top priority assigned to escort vessels in the British 1939 War Emergency, and 1940 Building Programmes. Moreover, the British had reintroduced convoy as soon as the war began—but the Japanese only adopted convoy in November 1943, having lost 22 warships and 296 merchantmen (total tonnage 1,335,240) in that year alone. At the same time the Japanese brought in an emergency escort-building programme—far too late to save their dwindling merchant fleet.

As for anti-submarine weaponry and technology, the threadbare and badly co-ordinated Japanese escort forces were pathetically ill-equipped. They relied on the depth-charge, supplemented by an Army trench mortar installed before the bridge. In the field of submarine detection, the Japanese Navy was still in the hydrophone era of World War I. About the only asset enjoyed by Japanese submarines was the excellent 'Long Lance' torpedo, one of the best weapons of the war. This travelled at 40 knots and was driven by liquid oxygen, leaving no track. But this was largely negated by the Japanese failure to use their submarines as an independent offensive arm. They never attempted pack tactics but tended to fritter away their submarine strength on lone gun bombardments of American atolls, or as communications ships, or as tankers for flying-boats. Another telling example of how Japanese sub-

marine development had become stuck at 1918 was their persistence with aircraft-carrying submarines, long after the British and Germans had given up submarine monitors and cruisers. The Japanese 'I-400' class aircraft-carrying submarines were the biggest boats ever built

Top: American 'T' class submarine. Above: The last seconds of a diminutive Japanese freighter.

Left: American *Gato* class.
Below: Japanese 'I-400' class.

before the nuclear era; but there was little these 3530-ton behemoths could achieve and they had hardly more than curiosity value in the Pacific War.

The courage, dash and skill of the American submariners was backed by a firm strategic understanding of what submarines were for, and how they could best be deployed against the Japanese Empire. The American equivalent of Dönitz in the Southwest Pacific, Rear-Admiral James Fife, urged his submarine commanders to 'press home all attacks'. His standing orders continued: 'Pursue relentlessly, remembering that the mission is to destroy every possible enemy ship. Do not let cripples escape or leave them to sink—make sure that they do sink.'

An important American contribution to the development of commerce warfare was the use of submarine-borne radar to locate targets. The most prestigious kill inflicted on a radar-located target was made early on the morning of 29 November 1944 by Commander Enwright of the *Archerfish*, who fell in with the giant new carrier *Shinano* (64,800 tons) making her first shakedown sea cruise. After a six-hour chase Enwright fired a salvo of six torpedoes, all of which hit. Though it is only fair to point out that

*Shinano*'s subsequent loss was due to inept handling on the part of her commander, she remains the heaviest warship ever to have been sunk by a submarine.

The campaign against the Japanese merchant fleet went from strength to strength in 1944. During that year American submarines accounted for 545 ships (2,140,000 tons). Tankers were the main prey at the beginning of the year and the record was held by Commander Dykes of *Jack*. On 19 February *Jack* encountered a small convoy of five tankers in the South China Sea and sank four of them in a running battle lasting all day. In April the US Pacific submarines were ordered to concentrate on Japanese destroyers. Hair-raising tactics were adopted to this end, such as the cold-blooded 'down the throat' shot—deliberately courting a ramming attack on the surface, and torpedoing the destroyer as it came in for the kill. No less demanding in skill was the 'up the kilt' shot: surfacing in the wake of a hunting destroyer and torpedoing it up the stern. The campaign against the Japanese destroyers was a resounding success: 39 of them had been sunk by submarines by the end of the war. The palm was won by Commander Dealey of *Harder* (lost with his

Opposite and below: Surrender of the giant, aircraft-carrying Japanese 'I-400' submarines in 1945.

With the Americans.
Left: Captain at the
periscope. Opposite, top:
Diving officer and planes-
men. Opposite, below: Crew
quarters, forward torpedo-
room. Below: Sinking
Japanese merchantman,
photographed through the
periscope of USS *Aspro*.

ship in August 1944) who sank three destroyers in three days in June 1944.

The Americans took enthusiastically to group attacks, particularly after the Pacific submarine base was moved west from Pearl Harbor to Saipan in August 1944. American 'wolf-packs' were smaller than the German ones and were used more for target location rather than actual attack. As was the German practice, American 'wolf-packs' took the name of their senior officer, though with typical American flamboyance—'Blair's Blasters', and the like. But

they had plenty to be flamboyant about. In June 1945 it was 'Hydeman's Hellcats' (nine boats led by Commander Hydeman in *Sea Dog*) who penetrated the inland Sea of Japan for the first time, carrying the sea war to Japan's door-step by sinking 27 Japanese merchantmen and the submarine *I-122* in 11 days.

By the time of the Japanese surrender in August 1945, the American submarine force in the Pacific had never risen above two percent of the massive naval forces deployed against Japan. But that two percent had sunk 240 Japanese warships and 2200 merchantmen—a grand total of $5\frac{1}{2}$ million out of the six million tons of merchant shipping with which Japan had entered the war, and one out of every three Japanese warships sunk. The deadly work of the American submarines had made it impossible for Japan to supply, reinforce and defend every bastion of the immense sea empire which she had conquered in 1941–42. No other weapon-system made such a one-sided contribution to Allied victory in World War II.

# 4. FROGMEN AND MIDGETS

No history of undersea war would be complete without mention of the handful of brave men, Axis and Allied, who volunteered for duty as underwater swimmers or as crew for human torpedoes or midget submarines. The sheer drama of their story, much of which could not be revealed at the time, provided a postwar crop of such paperback and cinema box-office successes as *The Frogmen* and *Above Us the Waves*. These 'special submarine operations', as they may be termed, introduced a unique level of selectivity into undersea warfare. They were, in fact, highly selective forms of mining carried out against anchored ships, with the explosive personally delivered to individual targets by means of specially designed vehicles. In all cases the latter were themselves carried to within striking distance by parent submarines, then released to penetrate the enemy anchorage under their own power.

These typical attack craft were of three basic types. First came the economical but extremely short-range 'human torpedo' with a two-man crew sitting on top. It carried to the target a warhead which was then detached and either fixed to the victim's hull or left underneath. The human torpedo was expendable; it lacked

the power to return to the open sea for a rendezvous with the parent submarine and the crew had the bleak choice of attempting to escape ashore or, as they were usually exhausted at the end of the attack, surrendering. There were two types of midget submarine whose crews travelled in a true submersible hull fitted with periscope and ballast tanks. One type fired torpedoes (from either single or double tubes, with no reloads); the other carried detachable charges for dumping beneath the target. Against warship targets the latter was vastly preferable because it guaranteed extensive damage to the target's bottom, whereas there was always a chance that a torpedo hit could be dissipated by armour or defensive 'bulging'. At the end of World War II the Germans introduced a third variant: one-man or two-man midget submarines (*Biber* and *Seehund*) carrying two torpedoes slung outside the hull.

Paradoxically, the first countries to plan special submarine operations were those which made the worst use of the orthodox submarine in World War II: Italy and Japan. John P Holland, the American submarine pioneer, had sketched a midget submarine back in the 1890s, but the first special attack craft to be seriously

Previous pages: British two-man 'chariot' on the surface. Below: The target which human torpedoes and midget submarines were designed to reach and destroy—a capital ship in her lair, safe from conventional submarine attack behind torpedo nets. This is the pocket-battleship *Lützow* (formerly *Deutschland*), sister-ship of *Graf Spee*, in a Norwegian fjord.

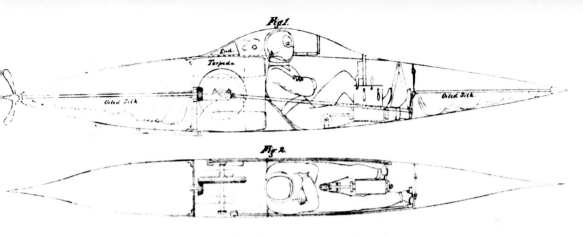

proposed took shape in Italy. In October 1935 two young Italian naval architects, T Tesei and E Toschi, submitted plans for the first human torpedo—the *Siluro a lenta corsa* (SLC) or 'slow-course torpedo'. A working prototype had been built and tested at La Spezia by the end of 1936 and a special department—Group H—undertook research and training until Italy's entry into the war on 10 June 1940.

The role envisaged for the SLCs, or *maiali* ('pigs'), as they were nicknamed, was that of clandestine attacks on the British naval bases at Gibraltar, Malta and Alexandria, and submarines were duly modified to carry the SLCs. From the beginning a long string of costly failures did nothing but reveal the hazards of the concept when put into practice. The first attempt was made in late August 1940: a raid on Alexandria, with the submarine *Iride* carry-ing three SLCs. This ended in fiasco on 22 August when *Iride* was spotted in the Gulf of Bomba and sunk by aircraft from the carrier *Eagle*. But the secret of the SLCs was still intact and a double operation was planned for September, with *Sciré* carrying SLCs to attack Gibraltar, and *Gondar* was similarly equipped to attack Alexandria. *Sciré* found no worthwhile

Above: Nothing if not imaginative, though nearly 50 years before its time. John P Holland's sketch for a one-man 'Submarine Torpedo-Boat' was done in the 1890s when his first submarines had yet to enter service. Kopechy's midget submarine idea (left) was of the same vintage. Below: Submarines and midgets in A Robida's visionary 'War in the Twentieth Century', published in Paris in 1887.

The Italians were the first to demonstrate what human torpedoes could do, sinking the British battleships *Valiant* and *Queen Elizabeth* at Alexandria in December 1941. Top: Captured specimens are tried out by Allied operators after the Italian surrender in 1943. Above: Hoisting out one of the streamlined, later Italian craft.

SLCs. Persistence with the SLC programme indicated rather the failure of the Italian Navy to introduce a coherent operational programme with their orthodox submarines. The risk of one or more SLCs being captured and examined was extremely high and the Italians were lucky that the SLCs' existence remained a secret until the summer of 1941.

When the secret was revealed it was in spectacular fashion. On the night of 25–26 July 1941 the Italians attempted a combined attack on the naval base at Malta. It was an extraordinarily audacious plan, reflecting highly on the morale and courage of the Italian naval volunteers. High-speed explosive motorboats were to blast breaches in the protective booms and nets, allowing two SLCs to penetrate the harbour. Radar alerted the British defences and the attack was smashed; one of the SLC crews blew themselves up with their craft, but the other was salvaged and examined. Even this disaster did not lead to the abandonment of the SLC programme and persistence finally won its reward on 20 September 1941, when the tanker *Denbydale* was badly damaged in Gibraltar by an SLC charge fixed to the bilge keel. This, the first successful human torpedo attack, was carried out by Visintini and Magro, launched from *Sciré*.

The most famous human torpedo attack of the war was also launched from *Sciré*, two months later—the sinking of the British battleships *Queen Elizabeth* and *Valiant* in Alexandria on the night of 18–19 November 1941. Three SLCs penetrated Alexandria, two of which laid their warheads correctly. The attack commander, Count Luigi de la Pene, was captured with his second in command, Bianchi, and interrogated aboard *Valiant* while the warhead's time-fuse was still running. As they would give nothing away, they were imprisoned deep in the battleship until de la Pene, knowing that nothing the British did now would be of any use, sent Captain Morgan the message 'Your ship will blow up in five minutes.' The Italians were on deck when the two battleships shook to violent explosions and settled on the harbour bed. They were as sunk as ships could be in such shallow water, and the Italian Navy now had the domination of the Mediterranean within its grasp—but this supreme opportunity was wasted. Both battleships still had their decks well above water, and were able to simulate readiness for sea by emitting funnel smoke. With the four men from the other two SLCs all captured ashore, it was not until

targets at Gibraltar and returned to base; *Gondar* had no better luck at Alexandria but was depth-charged and sunk on her return journey. Although the SLC crews were captured with *Gondar*'s crew the British learned nothing about the SLC programme and a further attempt on Gibraltar was made in November 1940, again with *Sciré*. This time a rich prize was spotted in Gibraltar: the battleship *Barham*. Two of *Sciré*'s three SLCs broke down after launching; their crews scuttled the SLCs and escaped into Spain. The crew of the third, piloted by Lieutenant Birindelli, nearly succumbed to oxygen poisoning from their highly dangerous breathing apparatus, but not before Birindelli, on the verge of unconsciousness, had dragged his SLC to within 30 yards of the *Barham*.

The Italians deserve the highest credit for continuing with SLC operations after these initial failures, but it should be pointed out that this was not solely due to unshakeable faith in months later that the Italian *Comando Supremo* learned what a chance had been missed.

To such attacks the British had no answer apart from constant vigilance and the formation of special diving parties to search ships' bottoms for unexploded charges. The first of these groups was the UWWP (Under-Water Working Party) formed at Gibraltar under Lieutenants 'Bill' Bailey and 'Buster' Crabb, who in 1941 had nothing better to work with than the Davis emergency breathing gear used for escaping from sunken submarines.

Another mode of attack pioneered by the Italian Navy was inspired by the unique geography of Gibraltar and the friendly neutrality of Spain: the underwater swimmers of 'Group Gamma', operating from Algeciras across the bay. They carried special mines supported by inflatable rubber rings, each supporting a five-pound charge. The swimmers operated from an interned Italian ship, the *Folgore*, and scored their first success on 14 July 1942 by damaging three British merchantmen in Gibraltar. Another interned ship, the *Olterra*, was used as an even more subtle 'Trojan Horse' by the Italians. Her bows were modified to create a special underwater compartment from which SLCs could be launched and proceed directly across the bay to Gibraltar. The first SLC attack from

the *Olterra* (7 December 1942) was another fiasco. The three craft were spotted during the approach; one was damaged by depth-charges, the second came under machine-gun fire and returned to the *Olterra*, and the crew of the third was killed by explosive charges. The latter crew was the veteran partnership of Visintini and Magro, who had carried out the first successful attack on the *Denbydale* in the previous year. It took until May 1943 before enough parts and personnel had been smuggled through Spain to the *Olterra* for another three-craft attack on Gibraltar.

The *Olterra*'s secret was so closely guarded that the Italian Foreign Office had no idea of what was afoot—let alone the fact that naval personnel had discreetly burgled the Foreign Office, purloining the diplomatic seal in order to safeguard the packages of SLC parts and breathing-gear on their way to Spain. But this extraordinary gamble yielded perfect results. On 8 May three SLCs evaded the British patrols and fixed their charges to three merchant ships at Gibraltar, sinking one of the ships and badly damaging the other two. All three SLCs returned safely to the *Olterra*. But the time and stealth needed to supply replacement parts meant that there could only be time for one more attack (in August), before the Italian surrender. This

'Hospital care' in dry dock reveals the massive damage done to *Valiant*'s bottom plating by de la Pene's devastating attack.

Above: British chariot of the type used in the abortive attempt to sink *Tirpitz* in October 1942. Opposite, top: Found in one of the Japanese midget submarines lost off Oahu was this detailed map of the US Pacific Fleet's anchorage, with positions of the major targets in 'Battleship Row' correctly scrawled in to the north of Ford Island. Opposite, below: Japanese Type C midget submarine (No 69) embarked on a transport at Kure in August 1944. The Japanese persistence with torpedoes as the main armament for their midget craft meant that the tubes took up half the length of the boat.

time three ships were sunk: two cargo ships and a 10,000-ton tanker. As the SLCs returned to the *Olterra* they had the luck to be screened from observation by a timely school of porpoises going their way.

The courage and persistence of the Italian SLC men caused the British to revise their somewhat negative opinion of the Italian Navy, but it was the attack on *Valiant* and *Queen Elizabeth* at the end of 1941 which proved that capital ships could be 'taken out' by human torpedoes no matter how safe or remote their anchorages might appear to be. Then, at the beginning of 1942, the German battleship *Tirpitz* entered service and moved north to Norway. As the entire capital ship deployment of the Royal Navy was dominated by the threat posed by the *Tirpitz*, her elimination was of the highest priority. As neither the Home Fleet nor RAF Bomber Command could reach *Tirpitz* or hurt her, hopes were pinned on an attack with human torpedoes.

Under the stimulus of wartime urgency the British achieved in early 1942 what the Italians had taken five years to produce—a workable two-man human torpedo, known to the British as the 'chariot'. The *Tirpitz* remained the prime target, but the problem of getting chariots to within range of her were immense. It was not just the distance across the North Sea, but the long and tortuous passage up Trondheim fjord to the battleship's anchorage. After months of watchful reconnaissance checks and liaison with the Norwegian resistance, the fishing-boat *Arthur* set off from Shetland on 26 October 1942, carrying two chariots which were subsequently put over the side and towed. With the chariot crews hidden in the hold the skipper, Leif Larsen of the Norwegian resistance, bluffed his way past the German patrols and entered

Trondheim fjord—but with barely ten miles to go it was found that both chariots had broken free and were lost. There was nothing for it but to sink *Arthur* and make for the Swedish frontier. All made it but for A B Evans, wounded and captured near the frontier, and subsequently shot.

Further operations against the *Tirpitz* were suspended until the more versatile 'X-Craft' midget submarines were ready, but the British chariots continued in active service. On 3 January 1943 the Italians had their own weapon turned against them when three British chariots attacked Palermo, sinking the unfinished new light cruiser *Ulpio Traiano* and badly damaging the transport *Vimina*. On 18-19 January an attack by two chariots narrowly failed to prevent the Germans from sinking blockships to deny the facilities of Tripoli harbour to the advancing 8th Army. One of the chariot crews was captured, but the other two men managed to escape to the British lines. On the eve of the invasion of Sicily in July, chariots were frequently used to reconnoitre likely landing-beaches. But the biggest success for the chariots came three weeks after the fall of Rome in June 1944. A single chariot forced its way through dense anti-submarine nets into La Spezia harbour and sank the last Italian heavy cruiser, *Bolzano*, which the Germans had seized at the time of the Italian surrender and withdrawn to the north.

The first true midget submarines, those of Japan, had been developed (like Italy's SLCs) in the late 1930s. The *Ha*-boats, as they were known, were two-man craft and their biggest design fault was the use of twin torpedo tubes, mounted one above the other in the bow. This offered the chance of attacking two separate targets, but as the tubes took up half the size of the boat there was only room for an electric motor aft, which in turn yielded a very limited operational radius (about 80 miles at a submerged speed of two knots). Five *Ha*-boats were committed to the attack on Pearl Harbor in December 1941, being carried within striking range by parent submarines. But none of them got close enough to attack or even sight the neat line of American battleships moored two by two in Battleship Row. Two met unknown fates; the other three were accounted for well in advance of the Japanese air strike, falling victim to the destroyers *Ward*, *Monaghan* and *Helm*—the latter forcing *Ha-19* to beach herself.

Despite this initial fiasco at Pearl Harbor, the great range of Japanese submarines permitted the launching of the most ambitious midget submarine operation ever made. On 30–31 May 1942, ten *Ha*-boats struck virtually simultaneously at Diego Suarez in Madagascar and at Sydney in Australia. The timing of these widely separated attacks was intended as a diversion from the imminent Japanese assault on Midway in the central Pacific (which, thanks to brilliant code-cracking and detective work from radio intercepts, the Americans already knew would be the next main target for the Japanese). But the Diego Suarez attack gave Japan's midget submarines their biggest success of the war. It was preceded by an air reconnaissance flight by a seaplane launched from the submarine *I-10*. This alerted the Allies in Diego Suarez but did not save the British battleship *Ramillies* from severe damage, while a tanker was sunk. The American heavy cruiser *Chicago* was in Sydney Harbour when eight *Ha*-boats attacked on the night of 31 May, but the only torpedo to come her way hit and sank an old ferry boat commandeered as an accommodation ship.

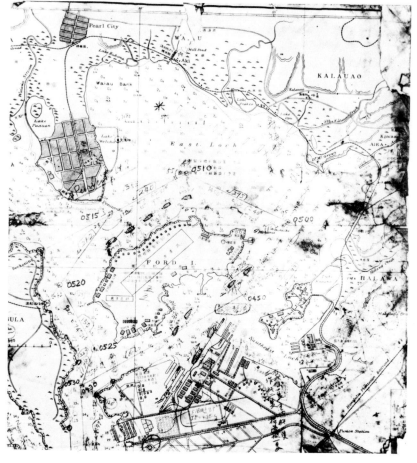

German *Biber* one-man midget submarine.

As happened in Germany to the considerable benefit of the Allies, Japan's naval construction throughout the war suffered from confused priorities and persistence with a multiplicity of types which ate up scarce raw materials, manpower and building facilities. The 77th *Ha*-boat, first of the improved 'Type D', was not completed until January 1945. It was scheduled for a mass production of 540 boats, but the days when the US Pacific Fleet and its allies operated from 'fixed addresses' suitable for midget submarine attack were long gone. Ever since the Pearl Harbor attack over three years before it had been evident that Japanese midget submarine operations were, in effect, suicide operations. Although there was never any lack of eager human volunteers, the production of such sophisticated machines was a profligate waste. Over the last few months of the war, when American B29 Superfortress raids ruined the 'Type D' building schedule, the Japanese at last turned from midget submarines to true suicide craft: the *Kaiten* manned torpedoes and *Shinyo* explosive speedboats.

It was the British who produced the most effective midget submarine of the war: the four-man 'X-craft' with diesel-electric power. One of the crew was a diver who could leave and re-enter the boat by means of a flooding chamber when required for cutting nets or clearing obstacles. Attacks were carried out by working the boat directly under the target's hull, then dumping the fused explosive charges carried outside the X-craft's hull, sending out the diver to fix magnetic limpet mines to the target, or both. A true war-child, the X-craft was developed after the Italians (at Alexandria) and Japanese (at Diego Suarez) had given convincing demonstrations that capital ships could be attacked, crippled and even sunk at anchor by

special attack craft. Despite no previous experience with the type, the British produced a workable prototype by the end of 1942 and on 17 April 1943 formed the 12th Submarine Flotilla to train for midget submarine operations. There could be no doubt what its first objective would be: the daunting concentration of capital ships assembled by the Germans in Arctic waters. This concentration, which obliged the British to suspend the sailing of convoys to north Russia during the summer of 1943, consisted not only of the battleship *Tirpitz* but of the battlecruiser *Scharnhorst* and pocket-battleship *Lützow*.

As with the abortive chariot attack on the *Tirpitz* in October 1942, intense preparations were needed before the first X-craft attack could be launched. The problem of target location and confirmation had intensified when the Germans moved their heavy ships north to Altenfjord at Norway's northern tip, and a special flight of reconnaisance Spitfires was sent to north Russia to obtain up-to-date photographs of the German ships in their anchorages. Then there was the problem of the long approach to Altenfjord from northern Scotland, finally solved by towing each X-craft behind a submarine. During the approach a passage crew aboard each X-craft kept the tiny craft in operational order, with the attack crew transferring when the moment came to part company with the parent submarine.

In the event six X-craft were dispatched: *X5*, *X6* and *X7* to attack the *Tirpitz*, *X8* to attack the *Lützow*, and *X9* and *X10* to destroy the *Scharnhorst*. The six submarines sailed with their charges in tow on 11–12 September 1943. The attacking force lost two X-craft at the outset: *X9* broke her two moorings and was never seen again; *X8* suffered similar misfortune but was recovered only to be proved unoperational due to air escapes. *X10* never did find the *Scharnhorst* (the battle-cruiser had moved down Altenfjord from her anchorage to carry out gunnery exercises) and *X10* eventually returned to sea, her crew being the only one to be recovered by one of the parent submarines. *X5* was never seen again after the 20th and was almost certainly the midget submarine which the Germans claimed to have sunk outside the nets screening the *Tirpitz*. But both *X6* and *X7* penetrated the *Tirpitz*'s net defences and jettisoned their charges beneath the hull, despite mechanical failures which obliged both craft to be scuttled and their crews to surrender, and despite being spotted and coming under enemy fire.

A torpedo
launched by a torpedo—
German special attack craft
*Neger*.

With the crew of *X6* captive aboard the
*Tirpitz*, there occurred an eerie re-play of the
scene aboard the *Valiant* in Alexandria in
November 1941. Like de la Pene and his second
in command, Lieutenant Donald Cameron and
his crew counted the seconds until their explosive charge was due to detonate. Meanwhile the
Germans, with no steam raised to permit an
instant shift of anchorage and no tug handy,
altered *Tirpitz*'s berth as much as they could by
hauling in her anchor cable. This moved her
away from *X6*'s charges but not from the second
charge dropped by *X7*, which exploded under
the battleship's engine-room. The *Tirpitz* lay

immobilised until the spring of 1944, permitting
the re-starting of the Russian convoys and the
successful interception and sinking of the
*Scharnhorst* by Admiral Sir Bruce Fraser and
the Home Fleet on 26 December 1943.

No other midget submarine attack ever
reaped such immediate strategic benefit, but the
attack on the *Tirpitz* was by no means the last
X-craft operation in Norwegian waters. On
24 April 1944 *X24* was towed across the North
Sea to Bergen by the submarine *Sceptre*,
penetrated the harbour and sank the blockade-
running merchantman *Barenfels*, escaping to
sea for a successful rendezvous and return

Above: 'The victors of Hawaii'—German propaganda indulging in more than a little wishful thinking on behalf of the Japanese Navy. The Japanese had great hopes for their midget submarines, but their attempt to penetrate Pearl Harbor in December 1941 was a dismal failure. Opposite, Rear-Admiral Barry takes a 'ride' on one of his X-craft.

Opposite, below:
An X-craft diver cuts a hole in an anti-submarine net: a terrifying ordeal in pitch-black waters, with the submarine bumping and grinding against the meshes.

home. *Sceptre* and *X24* (the latter commanded by Lieutenant H Westmacott in place of Lieutenant 'Maxie' Shean, her captain on the first attack) paid a return visit to Bergen on 11 September 1944, sinking the large floating dock which had escaped her in April. X-craft also put in sterling work during the reconnaissance of the Normandy beaches before the landings on 6 June and were used to guide the assault forces in to the beaches.

For the X-craft and their dedicated crews it was ironic that just as they were reaching peak efficiency, and as the British transferred their main naval effort to the Pacific, the war in that theatre was proceeding so much in the Allies' favour that there was no longer full scope for midget submarine operations. The last great surface battle of the Pacific War had been fought at Leyte Gulf in October 1944, and by the summer of 1945 no dangerous concentration of Japanese capital ships survived as a suitable target for midget submarine attack.

Nevertheless, the improved 'XE-craft' sent to the Pacific succeeded in making their mark. In late July the submarines *Spark* and *Stygian* towed *XE3* and *XE1* from Brunei to Singapore for an attack on the Japanese cruisers *Takao* and *Myoko*, which represented a potential threat to the operations being planned for the liberation of Malaya. Lieutenant Ian Cameron's *XE3* successfully attacked the *Takao* after an epic performance by the diver, Leading Seaman

Magennis, who had the greatest difficulty in fixing the limpet mines to the *Takao*'s growth-encrusted bottom plating. Once the limpets were placed the detachable charges were fused and slipped but the starboard carrier jammed fast, obliging the already tired Magennis to go out again and lever it clear. Even then *XE3*'s troubles were not over, for it was impossible to maintain a correct trim in the fresh water of the Johore Strait, and at one stage *XE3* broke surface in sight of the *Takao*. Overcoming all difficulties, *XE3* nevertheless completed her withdrawal and rendezvous with *Stygian*. Meanwhile Lieutenant Smart of *XE1*, unable to find the *Myoko*, made the courageous decision to shift his target and attack the *Takao* as well, accepting the risk that *XE3*'s charges might already be in place with their fuses activated. He, too, attacked the *Takao* and withdrew successfully. The double set of charges sank the *Takao*. Though not completely submerged, she was finished as a seagoing fighting ship.

At the same time as the attacks at Singapore, two other XE-craft embarked on a highly significant mission: to locate and cut the undersea cable communications between the Asian mainland and the outlying Japanese bases. This was successfully accomplished off Saigon and Hong Kong—an achievement too late to have any dramatic effect on the outcome of the Pacific War, but a demonstration of midget submarine potential of the highest significance for the future.

Finally, mention should be made of the despairing German attempt to create a miniature U-boat fleet to stave off the invasion of Europe. In total contrast to the success of the British X-craft and XE-craft, this belated German effort mirrored the multiplicity of types, waste of resources and negative results of the Japanese programme. The basic starting-point of German midget craft design was a torpedo slung beneath a torpedo from which the warhead had been removed, and to which a primitive cockpit and controls had been added. This produced the *Marder*, capable (unlike the smaller *Neger*) of running submerged; and the heavier *Hecht*, which was grandly designated the 'U-XXVII' class. True midget submarines were developed in the form of the one-man *Biber* and two-man *Seehund*, each type carrying a brace of torpedoes slung outside the hull. All these were produced in large numbers in the feverish expectation of spectacular results but the latter failed to materialise because the German planners had misunderstood the true

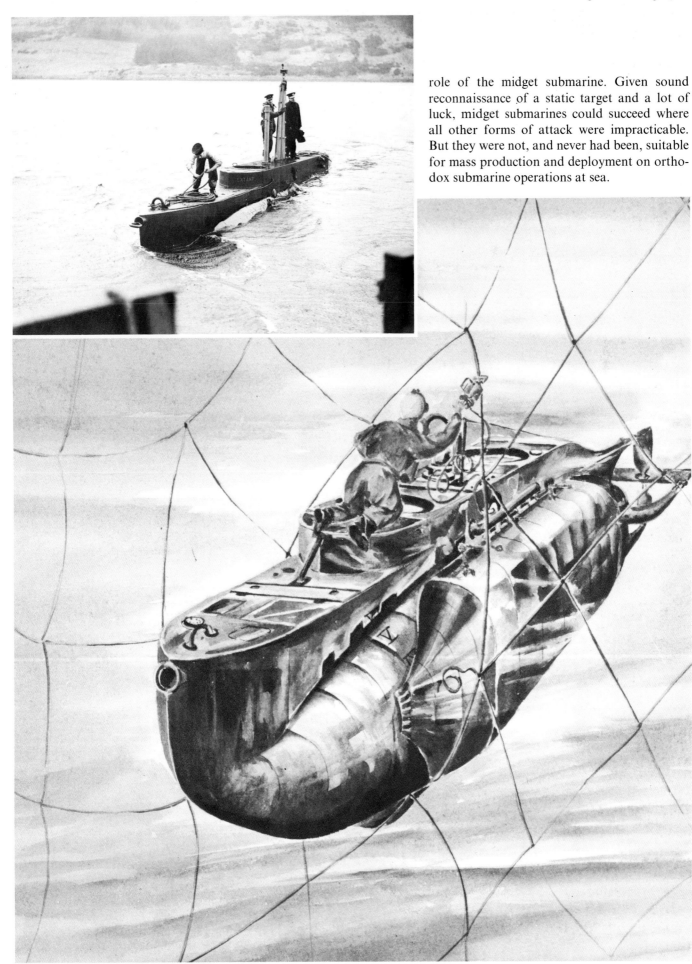

role of the midget submarine. Given sound reconnaissance of a static target and a lot of luck, midget submarines could succeed where all other forms of attack were impracticable. But they were not, and never had been, suitable for mass production and deployment on orthodox submarine operations at sea.

# 5. BALANCE SHEET, 1945

As far as the undersea war was concerned, far more technological progress was made in World War II than in World War I. On land, sea, and in the air, World War II was the scientists' war. Their accumulative work on submarine design, submarine detection and the techniques of counterattack against submarines had, by 1945, transformed the comparatively crude submersible warships, which went to war little changed, in essentials, from those of 1914.

If the war had not ended in 1945, and if by some alchemy all the Axis and Allied improvements made by 1945 could have been distilled and mixed, a compound on the following lines would have been the result.

The submarine's old dependence on surface attacks (preferably with the gun), exploiting the superior speed conferred by the craft's diesels, was ancient history. Streamlined and running on *schnorkel*, the ocean-going submarine now had no need to surface at all. It could match the top speed of nearly every type of enemy escort vessel and could easily outpace the escorts when they cut their speed, reducing water turbulence and surface noise to get a clear sonar echo. The submarine now carried radar for target detection, plus radar-detection equipment capable of sensing the activity even of the narrowest-beam anti-submarine radar. It also carried over twice the number of torpedoes carried by the smaller boats at the beginning of the war. Torpedoes were now being mounted in lateral tubes, which meant that it was no longer necessary to aim the whole boat at the target during an attack. Along with this advantage

went automatic reloading gear for torpedoes, cutting down on crew fatigue and eliminating the old frustration of having to break off from the target in order to reload tubes for the next attack. The torpedoes themselves were sophisticated improvements on an old theme. As well as the original straight-and-level type there were now acoustic torpedoes, capable of hunting down a target by following its engine noises, and torpedoes which could be set to follow a jinking, unpredictable course, used for firing into the drilled ranks of enemy merchant convoys.

The submarine still lent itself admirably to the vital role of clandestine minelaying, unloading contact, magnetic or acoustic mines. But it was about to take on an entirely new strategic role: long-range bombardment by missile from 'no fixed address'. Between 1944 and 1945 the missile age had arrived. Accurate electronic guidance for missiles still lay in the future, but the Germans had proved that it was possible to fire a rocket missile across the North Sea and hit London. They had also proved that it was possible to launch such missiles from under water. Over the previous 20 years submarines had been proved capable of carrying and launching aircraft. By 1945 it was only a question of time before they were rendered capable of carrying surface-to-surface missiles: the pilotless-aircraft, cruise-missile type (of which the V1 'doodlebug' was the crude original) and the V2 rocket type. Before the war ended the Germans had been working on a plan to tow V2s to their launch-points in special firing tubes and launch them from

beneath the ocean's surface. Once the technique of submarine rocket launching had been proved feasible, the cities of the United States could no longer count themselves immune from long-range rocket bombardment launched by submerged submarines. This, the blueprint for Polaris, was one of the deadliest legacies of World War II.

As Schnee's Type XXI demonstrated on 30 April 1945, the advent of the high-speed submarine promised a rich crop of new problems for surface escorts. The great victory over the U-boats in May 1944 had been the victory of escorts over submarines without *schnorkel*, forced time and again to submerge and crawl along on their electric motors by ever-more-frequent Allied air patrols. But the high-speed submarine, operating submerged throughout its patrol, showed up the limitations of the escorts' detection equipment and weaponry. Shipboard radar was useless against submerged submarines and could not be relied upon to detect a *schnorkel* head, while shipboard sonar had a very short range and could no more detect a submarine approaching at speed just below the surface than could radar. Even at close range, high submerged speeds gave a sonar-detected submarine a better chance of breaking free from the sonar beam.

But from early 1944 two new Allied inventions came into service, opening a new era in the detection of submerged submarines. Both were for use by that ubiquitous, high-speed foe of the submarine—aircraft—and they were the Magnetic Air Detector (MAD) and the sono-buoy. Both are still very much in use in the 1980s.

MAD told a low-flying aircraft when it was flying over a submerged metal mass behaving like a submarine, and enabled the aircraft to track its quarry. The sonobuoy was a hydrophone-carrying buoy which could be dropped into the sea by a patrolling aircraft and left to get on with the job of listening for submarines without distracting surface and engine noises from a parent craft; if it heard suspicious submerged engine noises it notified the aircraft accordingly by radio. Since the hydrophone's introduction in World War I, the problem of a parent surface craft's own noises had made hydrophones better suited for use by submarines than surface vessels, which had to stop to make a listening search by hydrophone, thus making the parent craft a sitting target as well as drastically limiting the area which could be searched. But an aeroplane quartering its 'beat'

and periodically dropping sonobuoys could now search vast expanses of ocean. The only certain safeguard against hydrophone detection was for the submarine to remain stopped with its crew observing 'silent routine'. To this end the big new Type XXI submarines had been given silent 'creeping' electric motors, but even when proceeding with palsied stealth at speeds under five knots nothing could be done to eliminate the sound of a submarine's propeller.

Together, MAD and the sonobuoy spelled a breakthrough in submarine detection as big as the introduction of sonar in the late 1930s. Their most effective use (and one of the hardest to contrive in practice, even with the swarming surface forces available to the Allies in 1944–45) was close air/sea teamwork, the aircraft locating and engaging the submarine while directing surface vessels to the spot to join the attack and verify a 'kill'. Admittedly only 12 U-boats were sunk by air/sea attacks in the last 11 months of the war. But if Germany's new U-boat fleet of Type XXIs had managed to open a renewed offensive in the North Atlantic, MAD and the sonobuoy would have been vital tools of the Allied defensive.

Throughout World War II the leading anti-submarine weapon was, as in World War I, the depth-charge, thrown or dropped in 'wide' or 'close' patterns and given an ever-increasing choice of depth settings. The depth-charge was supplemented by forward-throwing mortars— 'Hedgehog' and its more formidable successor, 'Squid'—which gave the attacker more reach and countered the problem of deteriorating sonar echoes during the last stage of the attack. But the missile age had also extended to anti-submarine weaponry by the last year of the war. Against U-boats forced to remain on the

'Squid' forward-throwing mortar fitted in a British corvette in the latter months of World War II.

surface, one of the most potent weapons (as well as one of the most unlikely) was the rocket missile, fired in salvoes from beneath the wings of that obsolescent masterpiece, the Fairey Swordfish biplane. Germany was first in the field with an air-to-surface guided weapon, the SD1400 'Fritz X', one of which sank the Italian battleship *Roma* in September 1943. But the Americans had snatched the lead in air-to-surface anti-shipping missilery by the end of the war with the 'Bat', a winged missile, launched and steered to its target from a parent aircraft.

On its first operational trial, the Bat sank a Japanese destroyer at its extreme range of 25 miles. World War II therefore ended with the submarine facing the development of guided anti-submarine weapons.

When equipped with radar-detection gear and able to dive at once, a submarine had little to fear against orthodox air-to-surface missiles; but from the second half of 1943 the Allies had begun to deploy a worrying new anti-submarine weapon. This was the air-dropped acoustic torpedo, far more complex and expensive than the depth-charge, but much more effective against submarine commanders skilled in evading depth-charge attacks. The first success with the new weapon (known for security purposes as the 'Mark 24 mine') was scored on 3 July 1944 when a Liberator bomber of No 224 Squadron sank *U-514* off the northern coast of Spain. The aircraft in question was also the first to be fitted with a potent trinity of weapons—depth-charges, underwing rockets and the acoustic torpedo—used in succession to make certain of a 'kill'. Given time, miniaturisation and im-

'Very Long Range' Liberator bombers, based on Iceland, played a vital role in closing the 'Black Gap' in mid-Atlantic.

German air reconnaissance spots Convoy PQ17 as it forges confidently into the Barents Sea before the fatal 'scatter' order of 4 July 1942.

proved electronic control would marry the acoustic torpedo to the guided missile with devastating effect—the 'Asroc' missile of the 1970s—but the essential elements had been tried and tested in the latter months of World War II.

The experience of World War II also confirmed the need for constant vigilance and technological expertise in mine warfare. Germany's early deployment of the magnetic mine was a case in point. If the Germans had had abundant stocks of magnetic mines in September 1939—or had waited a few months before deploying them suddenly and in mass—the results on British shipping would have been calamitous. As it was, the speed with which the British countered the magnetic mine had two causes: prudence in peacetime, which meant that the British were already experimenting with magnetic sweeps by the outbreak of war, and sheer good luck in that an intact specimen was secured and examined as early as 22 November 1939. In the immediate aftermath of World War II, antimagnetic degaussing gear was a standard fitting in new merchant ships and continued to be encouraged in Britain by government subsidy until the early 1960s. The more subtle menace of the acoustic mine could only be countered by sweeping with a noise-making device. But, in general, World War II again proved that the mine—the 'second echelons' after the submarine of undersea war—had no superior as an inert agent of anonymous destruction at sea; and effective mine-hunting has remained an essential naval task since 1945.

Against submarine attack, both world wars established that convoy was the only long-term defence. In neither war were there sufficient numbers of U-boats to be unleashed *en masse* against Allied shipping at the outset of hostilities. This fact, so often overlooked, only underlines the vulnerability which every nation relying on seaborne imports should feel when a superpower starts building a massive submarine fleet—as the Soviet Union has done since the 1950s. For the World Wars also proved that it takes months before a nation's shipping habits are channelled into convoying its seaborne imports. The U-boats' initial heyday in 1939–40, as in 1915–17, was at the expense of independently sailed merchantmen because *convoy is only a wartime expedient*. It is impossible to switch the bulk of mercantile traffic from independent sailings to convoy with the wave of a wand on the outbreak of war.

The World Wars produced no alternative defensive strategy to convoy, which denies enemy submarines the easy meat of independent

victims and forces the submarines to come within reach of the hunter-killer forces hovering round the convoy. Nevertheless, the supreme crisis of early 1943 demonstrated that it was possible for a sufficiently large number of submarines to swamp a convoy's defences, even when the submarines were opposed by specialised weaponry and veterans of over two years' combat experience.

Apart from this sobering lesson, the convoy crisis of 1943 also proved the ineptitude of the German armed forces in combining the formidable resources at their disposal. Until 1943 the biggest Allied fear was that the German Navy would launch a simultaneous surface and submarine assault against the Atlantic convoys. It had taken an all-out effort by the Royal Navy to hunt down and sink the battleship *Bismarck* when she broke out into the Atlantic in late May 1941, during which month U-boat sinkings of merchant ships leaped from 43 ships (249,375 tons) in April to 58 ships (325,492 tons). Only three months before (23 January–22 March 1941) the *Scharnhorst* and *Gneisenau*, breaking out and operating together in the North Atlantic, had sunk or captured 22 ships (115,622 tons) and completely disrupted the Atlantic convoy cycle until they withdrew. At the beginning of 1943 the Germans had concentra-

ted such a powerful battle squadron in Arctic waters that the Allies were forced to suspend Russian convoys for the whole of that summer—but the suspension of the Russian convoys did not result in the battle squadron being switched to the North Atlantic route. In April 1943 even a feint by the German surface warships must have drawn off enough air and surface escort forces to have allowed the U-boats virtually a free hand against the North Atlantic convoys.

That this is no fanciful hypothesis is proved by citing the tragedy of Convoy PQ17 on the Russian route in early July 1942. This convoy, in good heart after keeping U-boats and *Luftwaffe* bombers at bay for over two days, was prematurely scattered when the British Admiralty feared that the German battle squadron had sortied to attack. Only eleven merchantmen got through to Archangel; 22 others, dutifully scattered all over the Barents Sea, were sunk (ten by U-boats and 12 by aircraft).

On a different level, the sad story of PQ17 is interesting because it was a rare instance of submarines being used to augment a convoy's defence. PQ17's escort included the submarines *P613* and *P615*, whose senior officer suggested that the submarines should deliberately stay on the surface if the convoy came under surface attack. In the words of Captain Jack Broome

of the *Keppel*, commander of PQ17's close escort, 'it made sense as a practical suggestion as to how he and his partner could best be used. If they dived on sighting the enemy they would be pinned down by their slow underwater speed, and lucky to get in a shot. If, on the other hand, they showed themselves on the surface, they would be what Hitler's few remaining warships wanted to see least; like two wasps in a car, they would be extremely distracting and irritating to the driver'. The incident also gave birth to one of the flashes of impromptu humour which never completely deserted the undersea war, even in its darkest hours—as the following exchange of signals shows:

From: Senior Submarine Officer
                To: KEPPEL
IN THE EVENT OF ATTACK BY HEAVY ENEMY SURFACE FORCES PROPOSE TO REMAIN ON THE SURFACE.

From: KEPPEL
           To: Senior Submarine Officer
SO DO I

Though World War II was modern history's first demonstration of the hideous meaning of 'total' war, vestiges of chivalry survived. In September 1939, for instance, *Kapitänleutnant* 'Vaddi' Schultze of *U-48* sent a radio message in clear language to Winston Churchill, as First Lord, to pick up the survivors of *U-48*'s latest victim, *Royal Sceptre*—although. *Royal Sceptre*'s radio operator had committed the technically hostile act of continuing to transmit a raider report. Such elaborate courtesy was understandable enough in the first months of the war, but even in 1945, transcending the bitterness of the Pacific fighting, truces could still be declared between the rival belligerents. A

PQ17: the slaughter. Above: A German U-boat lookout scans the wreckage-strewn water. Below: Still flying her anti-aircraft kite balloon, a PQ17 victim sinks by the head. Right: Survivors from the American merchantman *Carlton*, moments from rescue by a U-boat.

classic example was the case of the 11,249-ton Japanese merchantman *Awa Maru* in February 1945. The Japanese claimed that she was on a mission of mercy, carrying war refugees, food and other supplies for prisoners of war along the China coast and in Japan. All American submarines were ordered not to attack *Awa Maru* if encountered, but she was nevertheless torpedoed and sunk in the Taiwan Strait, with the loss of 2043 lives, by the submarine *Queenfish* (Commander Charles E Loughlin). The outcry over the *Awa Maru* disaster caused Commander Loughlin to be court-martialled after the war, and his defence echoed the dilemma facing the U-boat commanders who sank *Lusitania* and *Athenia*. Loughlin claimed that *Awa Maru* was not where she was supposed to be and was, moreover, proceeding at the suspiciously high speed of 17 knots in thick fog; he had thought she was a warship. Subsequent evidence indicated that the sinking was justified because *Awa Maru* was carrying strategic war materials in the form of tin ingots to Japan. As with the *Lusitania* and *Athenia* sinkings, the *Awa Maru* debate continues—minus the 2043 dead witnesses who lost their lives in her.

The message for the future is clear with regard to pleas for humanitarian conduct in submarine warfare: submarine training is no school for such conduct. In the final analysis all hopes, even all orders for the display of humanitarian behaviour come down to the rapid decision taken by the man at the attack periscope. His first instinct is survival for his ship and his crew. His second is to contribute to the destruction of the enemy's war effort by sinking enemy ships. And the combat experience of two World Wars has combined to push any other consideration firmly into third place.

When that combat experience is rendered down to present a balance-sheet of achievement and losses, the following data emerge.

Germany was the only continental land power to wage deliberate submarine campaigns against a global sea power—the British Empire—in each of the two World Wars. The U-boat arm went to war in 1914 and 1939 with roughly the same number of submarines capable of operating in the Western Approaches of the British Isles, about 20 in each case.

U-boat construction in World War I (355 boats built between 1914 and 1918) was dwarfed by the construction of World War II (1162 built between 1939 and 1945). In neither case did overall construction achieve genuinely efficient results, due to excessive experimentation and the retention of older types.

In World War I, U-boats sank 11,135,460 tons of Allied and neutral shipping, 4837 ships in all. The extremely large number of ships sunk was due to the fact that cargo-carriers of the time tended to be smaller and far more numerous than in World War II. (One regrettable byproduct of the U-boats' depredations in World War I was the virtual extinction of the sail carrying trade.)

The U-boats of World War II only sank 2828 ships but the overall tonnage was higher than in World War I: 14,687,231.

In World War I a total of 198 U-boats was lost (5354 officers and men). World War II losses were 784 boats lost (632 of them at sea), totalling 28,000 officers and men. World War II boats carried bigger crews than their World War I counterparts: while the 'Mittel-U' type of World War I had a complement of about 35, the Type VIIC of World War II crewed 44. Moreover, World War I U-boats were never exposed to the air attacks which cut increasingly heavily into World War II U-boat strengths.

Though the object of the U-boat campaigns was to sink Allied merchant ships rather than kill Allied merchant seamen, the grim result of unrestricted tactics was to render the two virtually synonymous. World War II losses for the British Merchant Navy alone are reckoned at 30,248 men.

The only other sea power to have waged a comparable submarine campaign was the United States, against the Japanese merchant fleet. Though faced with the strategic demands of a 'two-ocean' (Atlantic and Pacific) war, the USA deployed nearly all her submarines against the Japanese.

The USA entered the war in December 1941 with 67 submarines completed before 1926, and another 41 completed between 1926 and 1941. This gave the US Navy a most valuable training fleet, a facility which the German U-boat arm never enjoyed.

Between 1941 and the end of 1945 the Americans built 215 new submarines, all of them *Gato* class with the exception of 30 *Tench* class. This concentration on a single proven type was in total contrast to the German mania for experimentation and multiplicity of types.

Between December 1941 and August 1945, operating solely against Japanese and Japanese-controlled merchant shipping, US submarines

# WORLD WAR I: U-BOAT LOSSES

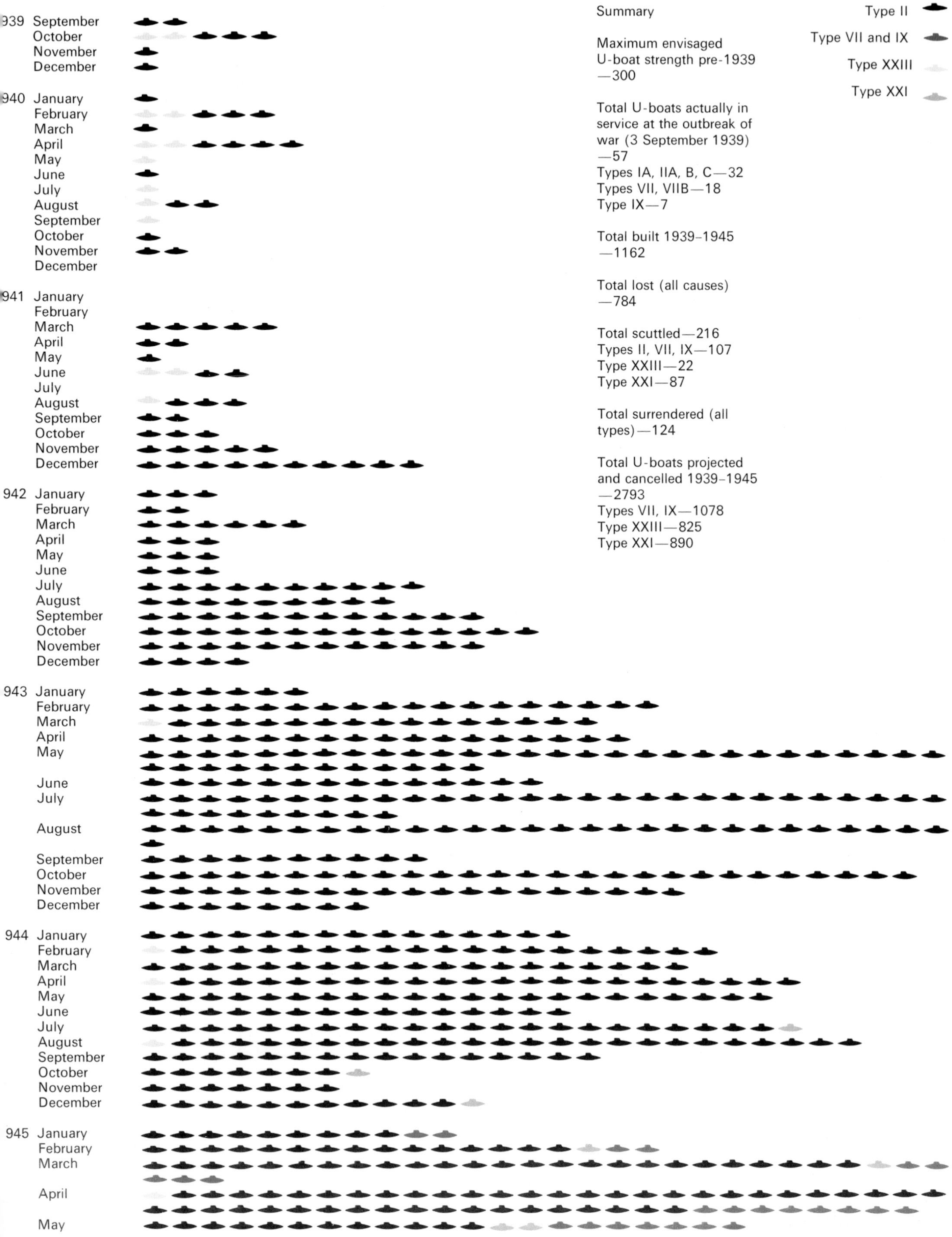

1939 September
October
November
December

1940 January
February
March
April
May
June
July
August
September
October
November
December

1941 January
February
March
April
May
June
July
August
September
October
November
December

1942 January
February
March
April
May
June
July
August
September
October
November
December

1943 January
February
March
April
May

June
July

August

September
October
November
December

1944 January
February
March
April
May
June
July
August
September
October
November
December

1945 January
February
March

April

May

Summary

Maximum envisaged
U-boat strength pre-1939
—300

Total U-boats actually in
service at the outbreak of
war (3 September 1939)
—57
Types IA, IIA, B, C—32
Types VII, VIIB—18
Type IX—7

Total built 1939–1945
—1162

Total lost (all causes)
—784

Total scuttled—216
Types II, VII, IX—107
Type XXIII—22
Type XXI—87

Total surrendered (all
types)—124

Total U-boats projected
and cancelled 1939–1945
—2793
Types VII, IX—1078
Type XXIII—825
Type XXI—890

Type II

Type VII and IX

Type XXIII

Type XXI

sank 1114 ships or 4,782,000 tons. When comparing these figures to sinkings by U-boats it should be remembered that the American *Gato* class displaced 1525 tons to the 769 tons of the Type VIIC, was armed with ten torpedo tubes to the six of the Type VIIC, and carried 24 torpedoes to the 14 of the Type VIIC.

American submarine losses totalled 49 boats (including 21 of prewar construction).

The nearest the British came to a submarine commerce war was in the Mediterranean, attacking the Axis convoys to North Africa; but the British boats in the Mediterranean had so many other tasks that no real parallel to the U-boat or American campaigns can be said to have existed. In September 1939 Britain had 57 submarines, and she built another 170 during the war. In the Mediterranean between June 1940 and December 1944, British and British-controlled submarines sank 286 ships (1,030,960 tons) for the loss of 52 submarines in that theatre. Overall British submarine losses for World War II amounted to 90 boats.

Such, then, were the levels which undersea war had reached by the end of World War II. Unlike the immediate aftermath of World War I, the coming of peace in 1945 held out no likelihood of any naval confrontation in the future. After 1918 the end of hostilities against Germany had merely sent the victorious Allies plunging head-on into another naval building race, before the Washington Naval Treaty of 1922 called a temporary halt. But in 1945 Germany and Japan were prostrate, ruined, and occupied by Allied troops. The fleets of the United States and Britain were supreme on every ocean of the world. And the Soviet Union, which had carried the heaviest burden of land fighting against Germany, possessed a threadbare fleet capable of little more than coastal defence.

Before Soviet truculence turned to open hostility with the Berlin blockade and the 'outbreak' of the Cold War, the Free World in 1945 can hardly be blamed by posterity for having failed to detect an ominous precedent and apply it to the Soviet Union. That precedent was Germany's rejection in the 1930s of a limited naval role, her gradual construction of a balanced and most formidable navy, finally building up the biggest submarine fleet the world had ever seen to challenge the sea powers who had brought her down in 1918.

Right: The blazing grave of a tanker.

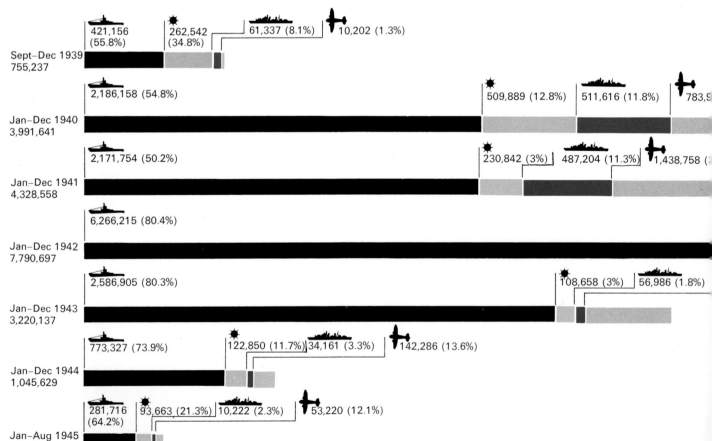

Sept–Dec 1939
755,237
421,156 (55.8%) 262,542 (34.8%) 61,337 (8.1%) 10,202 (1.3%)

Jan–Dec 1940
3,991,641
2,186,158 (54.8%) 509,889 (12.8%) 511,616 (11.8%) 783,9

Jan–Dec 1941
4,328,558
2,171,754 (50.2%) 230,842 (3%) 487,204 (11.3%) 1,438,758 (

Jan–Dec 1942
7,790,697
6,266,215 (80.4%)

Jan–Dec 1943
3,220,137
2,586,905 (80.3%) 108,658 (3%) 56,986 (1.8%)

Jan–Dec 1944
1,045,629
773,327 (73.9%) 122,850 (11.7%) 34,161 (3.3%) 142,286 (13.6%)

Jan–Aug 1945
438,821
281,716 (64.2%) 93,663 (21.3%) 10,222 (2.3%) 53,220 (12.1%)

**WORLD WAR II: BRITISH, ALLIED AND NEUTRAL MERCHANT SHIPPING LOSSES**
**(Gross tonnage)**

.6%)

104,588 (1.3%)  396,242 (5%)  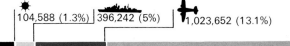 1,023,652 (13.1%)

588 (14.5%)

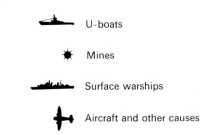

U-boats

Mines

Surface warships

Aircraft and other causes

# 6. NUCLEAR GENESIS, 1944-60

To the victor go the spoils; and for the Allies in 1945 the relative sophistication of Germany's last generation of World War II weaponry made those spoils rich indeed. The British overran Wilhelmshaven, Hamburg and Kiel, capturing not only the entire German naval archives but most of the technical information on the new U-boats. The Americans netted Wernher von Braun; other members of the German rocket programme were captured by the Russians. The advancing Russians had found leaner pickings in the captured German Baltic naval bases; but the Western Allies honoured their commitment to an even dispersal of all captured U-boats, an event which had the most profound effect on postwar submarine development.

A total of 156 operational U-boats had obeyed Dönitz's last order (4 May 1945) to surface, hoist the black flag and surrender. In addition to the U-boats which surrendered intact there were 221 others which had been defiantly scuttled by their crews; many of these could be salvaged. Finally there were scores of unfinished U-boat hulls and prefabricated U-boat sections still under construction at the moment of the German surrender, or abandoned because of bomb damage. Most of the latter were in the British sector. The basic share-out of intact U-boats was made on the basis of ten apiece to Britain, the United States and the Soviet Union; the rest were to be scrapped or sunk. In the New Year of 1946, 116 U-boats were sunk off Malin Head in Northern Ireland. Over the following year the Soviets tried to add to their quota by loading the unfinished German aircraft-carrier *Graf Zeppelin* with U-boat parts and equipment, but she hit a mine and sank while on tow to Leningrad in August 1947.

Apart from such refinements as automatic torpedo-loading gear, automatic depth-keeping gear (very necessary for taking the strain out of long runs at periscope depth), the *schnorkel* system, and radar-detection equipment, the biggest revelation was the source of high-speed power in the Type XXIs and Walter boats. The British had the luck to capture two operational prototypes of the Walter design (*U-1406* and *U-1407*). After handing over *U-1406* to the Americans they commissioned *U-1407* as HMS *Meteorite* and spent the next 12 years vainly trying to make Walter's explosive peroxide-based fuel into a safe operational proposition. As the Americans led the world with experience, money and resources for nuclear research they soon abandoned the Walter concept in favour of a nuclear power plant suitable for use in submarines. But all three of the navies which evaluated the Type XXI—British, American and Russian—wasted little time in adopting the Type XXI's best features to produce the next generation of diesel-electric submarines. And the spur for the latter development was the Berlin blockade, Russia's first detonation of an atomic bomb within four years of the Americans (1949) and the Korean War.

The basic receptacle of the Type XXI formula was a big streamlined hull carrying an electric battery double the size of those used to drive the electric motors of orthodox submarines. Increased hull size yielded a crop of further advantages: room to carry *two* or more electric engines, linked in tandem and room to carry more torpedoes and more electronic and automatic equipment were but two. Instead of phasing out their submarines of World War II vintage and courting the enormous cost of building new fleets of high-speed submarines, the Americans and British preferred the more economical alternative of converting their most modern types.

The Americans led the way with their GUPPY ('Greater Underwater Propulsive Power') programme, starting with 20 boats of the late wartime *Balao* class (improved *Gatos* with all-welded construction), and adding 15 boats of the *Tench* class. The boats were sliced in half through the engine room and a new 15-foot, 40-ton section was added amidships. The conversion was completed by a general cleaning-up: removal of the foredeck gun, and conversion of the traditional rounded conning-tower into a flattened, streamlined 'sail'. The Guppy conversions gleaned much valuable experience, yielding higher underwater speeds in the region of 15–17 knots, longer submerged voyages, and much greater manoeuvrability. They also proved able to dive to 600 feet. During the Korean War the *Tench* class Guppy *Pickerel* made an impressive run from Hong Kong to Pearl Harbor in 21 days without surfacing (1950). Two years later she demonstrated her manoeuvrability (not to mention the hardiness of her crew) by surfacing like a breaching whale from 150 feet at the spectacular angle of 48 degrees—one of the steepest surfacing angles ever attempted in cold blood.

The Americans quickly followed up their Guppy conversions with the six 'High Speed Attack' submarines of the *Tang* class, laid down in 1949–50 and all completed by the end of 1952. The *Tang*s pushed submerged speed up

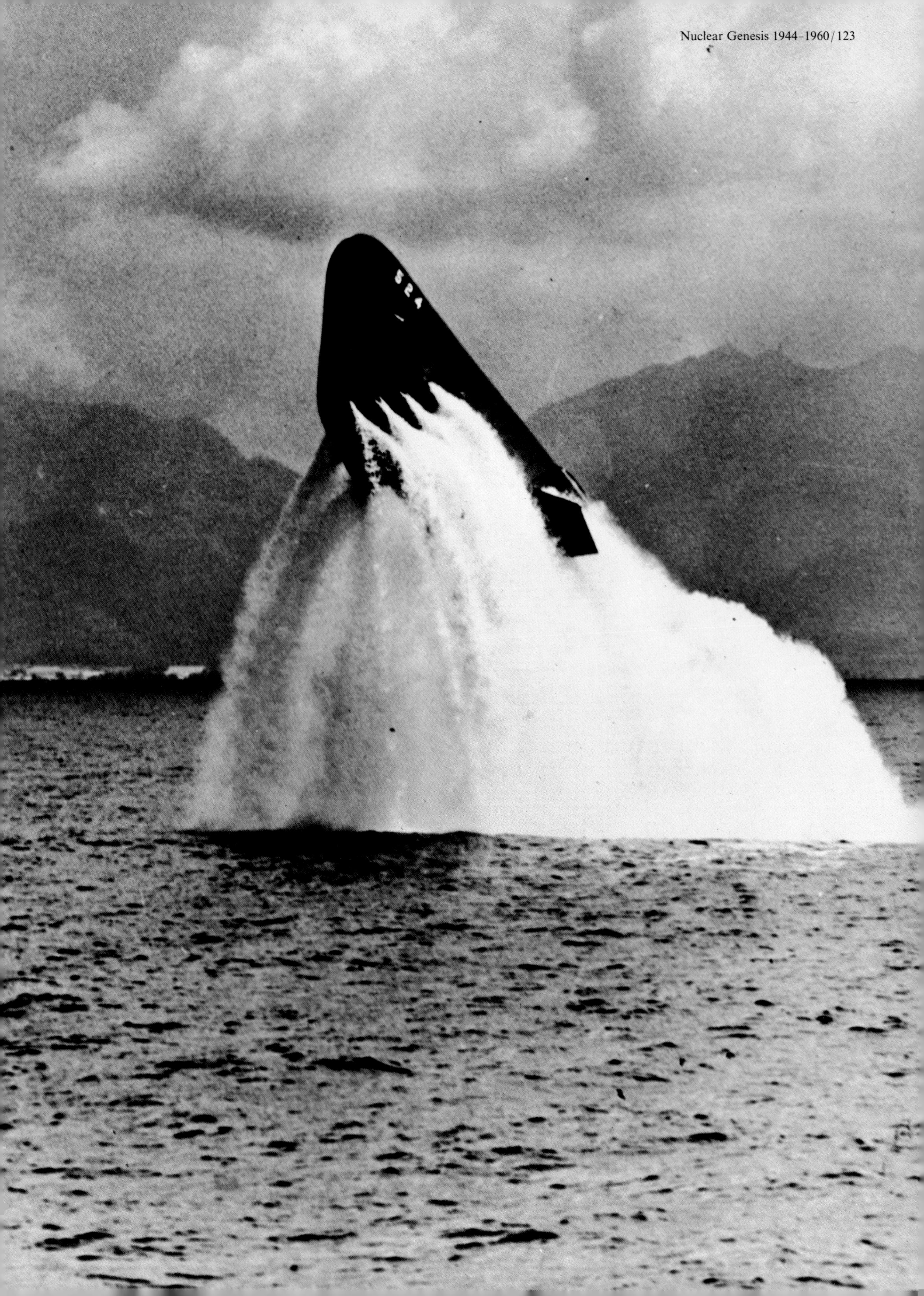

to 18 knots, still slightly below their best surfaced speed. Performance breakthrough was achieved with the 'High Speed Test Submarine' *Albacore*, an unarmed prototype designed and built to test the fully streamlined 'teardrop' hull. Completed in December 1953, *Albacore*'s top surfaced speed was 25 knots, with a submerged speed of 33 knots.

Thanks to the lessons learned from *Albacore* the Americans were able to push the diesel-electric submarine to the limits of its potential with the three *Barbel* class High Speed Attack submarines laid down in 1956–57 and completed in 1958–59. These featured the teardrop hull pioneered with *Albacore*, a surface speed of 15 knots and a submerged speed of 25 knots.

The speed with which the Americans were able to develop these successive designs, each one leading smoothly to improved performances with the next, was due to the American genius for planning and creating the most suitable infrastructure for long-term projects. (It was to be demonstrated to perfection in the following decade, with the Mercury/Gemini/Apollo space programme.) The underlying confidence behind the method was in turn a direct legacy of the war years, when brilliant organisation had fulfilled President Roosevelt's declaration that the United States should be 'the great arsenal of democracy'. And it explained why as early as June 1952—only three months after the experimental *Albacore* had been laid down—work could begin on the world's first nuclear-powered submarine, the USS *Nautilus*, launched on 21 January 1954. On 17 January 1955 a historic signal was flashed from Long Island Sound: UNDERWAY ON

## NUCLEAR POWER.

As might be expected with such a revolutionary concept, *Nautilus* was a prudent, 'belt-and-braces' design with three engine-room levels, for propulsion by nuclear, diesel or electric power. Her pressurised, water-cooled reactor of enriched uranium drove two-shaft Westinghouse turbines, delivering a surface speed of 20 knots and a submerged speed of 23 knots. *Nautilus* was given a conventional, though highly streamlined hull, capable of diving to 700 feet. Though in every way an experimental type on which the entire future of submarine design rested, *Nautilus* was also built as an operational warship armed with six forward torpedo tubes. To guarantee her the longest possible service life, she was also given a Guppy-type hull to facilitate the installation of improved power plants.

The nuclear power plant was revolutionary enough in itself—the biggest milestone in warship propulsion since the Parsons turbine

Opposite: The launching of USS *Nautilus*, 21 January 1954. Above: *Nautilus* in Long Island Sound, January 1955—'Underway on nuclear power' Left: High Speed Attack submarine, USS *Tang*.

began to supplant the reciprocating engine in the early years of the century. But when married to the weapons system of the submarine it opened a completely new era in undersea warfare. Nuclear power cut the submarine completely free from the surface, ending the need for the air-breathing advertisement of the *schnorkel*. It gave the submarine unheard-of range (*Nautilus* steamed 69,138 miles on her original reactor core, which was replaced for the first time in 1957) and meant that the only limit on the time the submarine could remain submerged was the endurance of her crew. For conventional surface warships armed with conventional anti-submarine weapons, the implications of a submarine able to maintain speeds of over 20 knots at depths of over 500 feet were horrendous. They made the old depth-charges

and mortar bombs of World War II seem like stone-age axes, and required new long-range sonar to detect this speeding menace in the depths. From her triumphant debut, less than ten years after American submarine designers had made their first examination of a Type XXI U-boat, *Nautilus* obliged every navy in the world to overhaul its anti-submarine defences and plan as best it could for a hazardous future.

The only serious setback to the new American nuclear submarine programme came with *Nautilus*'s successor, *Seawolf*, launched in July 1955. *Seawolf* was originally fitted with a liquid-sodium reactor instead of the pressurised-water type installed in *Nautilus*, but an ominous sequence of defects resulted in the removal of the original reactor and installation of a pressurised-water one. *Nautilus*, *Seawolf* and

Above: Successor to *Nautilus*—USS *Seawolf*.

all previous records by remaining submerged for 60 days while making a 15,700-mile cruise in the Atlantic (6 August–6 October 1958). In the same year *Nautilus* made the first submerged crossing of the Arctic Ocean, crossing the North Pole on 3 August. A year later (17 March 1959) *Skate* found a 'polynya', or temporary open seam in the solid pack ice, and surfaced at the North Pole. After these voyages, strategy for future naval wars had to include the potential for operations beneath the Arctic ice.

The nuclear revolution was necessarily accompanied by a new departure in submarine navigation, for there was no point in being able to remain submerged for weeks at a time if the submarine still had to surface regularly to take

their four successors—*Skate*, *Swordfish*, *Sargo* and *Snapdragon*, launched in 1957–58—established the 'first generation' of American nuclear submarines. They began to show the shape of things to come in 1958, when *Seawolf* shattered

optical sights for navigation. The new system, first given its public demonstration on *Nautilus* and *Skate*, is known as SINS—'Ship's Inertial Navigation System'. SINS uses electronic and engineering precision to take the error out of dead-reckoning navigation. It takes the precisely-known geographical starting-point of every voyage as the basis for all subsequent calculations of position, constantly applying every alteration of course and speed. The accuracy of SINS permits a margin of error no greater than 200-300 metres after a circumnavigation of the globe—all completely free from outside detection, or of the need to surface for optical or radio fixes.

America's 'first generation' of nuclear sub-

marines was rounded out by the six *Skipjack* class submarines, which were given the streamlined teardrop hull proven by *Albacore*. *Skipjack*, first of the class, was laid down in May 1956 and commissioned in April 1959; the other five had all been commissioned by the end of 1961. The *Skipjack*s broke the 30-knot barrier for submerged speed, but also served as a reminder of the prodigious cost involved in building a nuclear submarine fleet. *Nautilus*'s first reactor change had cost $20 million, but each of the *Skipjack*s cost $40 million to build.

The adoption of teardrop streamlining forced major rethinking in submarine armament, and hence in tactics. The pointed stern of the teardrop hull forced a concentration of the torpedo tubes in the bow; but the considerable increases in beam offered other possibilities. A World War II Type VII U-boat had a beam of about 16 feet; *Skipjack*'s beam was 31 feet. This gradual increase in beam led to the idea of mounting torpedo tubes laterally, able to fire to port and starboard instead of straight ahead. Such a facility would make possible a new breed of submarine: the 'submarine hunter-killer', or anti-submarine-submarine. Many times in the two World Wars, two enemy submarines had sighted each other on the surface or detected each other with hydrophones, and fallen into a tail-chasing circle. From its similarity to two dogs circling each other before coming to grips, British submariners had called this process 'doggy doggy'; it could only be broken by one submarine breaking off and escaping, or accidentally turning across the enemy's bow and stern tubes and exposing itself to torpedo attack. But a hunter-killer submarine armed with beam torpedoes would be ideally placed in such an encounter; and while *Skipjack* was still completing the Americans laid down the experimental *Tullibee*, commissioned in November 1960. She was the first submarine built with the bow position reserved for the active and passive sonar equipment needed for the detection and tracking of enemy submarines.

British postwar submarine development proceeded in a far lower key, without the political will, the money, or the nuclear research facilities enjoyed by the Americans. As the massive servicemen's vote indicated in the 1945 General Election, when Churchill was toppled from power, hopes for a brave new postwar world under a Labour government did not include restoring the Royal Navy as the world's strongest. Britain's economy had taken a terrible battering

Opposite: USS *Skipjack*, first nuclear submarine with the 'teardrop' hull pioneered by the experimental *Albacore*.

in World War II, which she had had to fight on credit. Britain was by far the biggest recipient of American financial foreign aid between 1945 and 1951, with a total of $6149 million in net grants and credits. (France came second, with $4328 million.) As the gradual conversion from Empire to Commonwealth proceeded through the 1950s and 1960s the Royal Navy retained a global role, but British submarine development came a poor second to maintaining the surface forces in the immediate postwar years.

The British long-term submarine programme after 1945 contented itself with applying the American Guppy technique to a selected number of wartime submarines. As the latter had always been smaller and slower than their American

contemporaries, it was hardly surprising that the performance of Britain's reconstructed submarines failed to reach the American level. The advantages of streamlining were frequently offset by the need to fit the cumbersome four-inch gun to submarines despatched to Commonwealth trouble spots.

Lack of funds for seaborne nuclear power research encouraged the British to continue tinkering with the Walter peroxide turbine system as a hopeful 'poor man's alternative' to nuclear power. As late as 1956–57 they were still prepared to lay down the experimental peroxide boats *Excalibur* and *Explorer*, the latter being known to her apprehensive crew as 'HMS *Exploder*'. The maximum performance claimed for *Excalibur* and *Explorer* was a precarious ten hours submerged at 27 knots, but the high consumption and dangerous instability of the fuel finally obliged the British to abandon the project in 1958.

By this date the first new British postwar submarines, the eight diesel-electric boats of the *Porpoise* class, were completing and the first

of 13 *Oberon*s had already been laid down. The best performance any of these boats could achieve was 12 knots surfaced and 17 knots submerged—a performance exceeded even by the American diesel-electric *Tang*s laid down some eight years before, and clearly inadequate for the nuclear era. Britain's decision to 'go nuclear' was made when the late Earl Mountbatten was First Sea Lord (1955–59). It was largely due to the relationship established by Mountbatten with Admiral Hyman Rickover, mastermind of the American nuclear submarine programme, that the British were allowed to purchase a complete nuclear power system for the first British nuclear submarine. This was HMS *Dreadnought*, a teardrop-hulled close

Opposite, top: 'HMS *Exploder'—Explorer*, Britain's experimental peroxide turbine submarine. Below left: HMS *Dreadnought*, Britain's first nuclear submarine. Below: *Dreadnought*'s captain at the periscope.

copy of *Skipjack*, laid down in 1959. When finally completed in the spring of 1963 she was given the peroxide-powered *Explorer* and *Excalibur* to use as high-speed underwater targets.

The Cold War began with Soviet land forces roughly matched in Europe, but with Soviet sea power derisory in comparison with that of Britain and the United States. This imbalance was clearly intolerable to the Soviet Union, obsessed with the security of its national territory after the terrible losses, human and material, of World War II. Stalin's decision to start building up a strong Soviet fleet was only to be expected, particularly after the formation of NATO (1949) and the awesome demonstra-

Below: British *Porpoise* class submarine, the first postwar diesel-electric design. Opposite: The long-serving *Oberon*s gave the British taxpayer excellent value for money.

Soviet 'Whiskey Twin-
Cylinder' submarine (the
cylinders housing her
missiles but making the
type very 'noisy' when
submerged), dressed overall
for Soviet Navy Day in
Sevastopol, August 1967.

tion of Anglo-American sea power in the
Korean War.

Stalin's naval building programme of 1950–51
makes an interesting comparison with the German naval 'Z-plan' of 1938–39. Both aimed at
the construction of balanced surface/submarine
fleets, but whereas Grand-Admiral Raeder had
envisaged a strong surface battleship/carrier
fleet capable of achieving parity with that of
the Royal Navy, the Soviet postwar programme
headed by Admiral Kuznetsov accepted that
the Soviet Union could never hope to match
the carrier strength of the West. To counter the
latter menace, Stalin approved the commence-
ment of the biggest submarine-building programme ever envisaged—not as a commerce-

destroying force, but as the only way of nulli-
fying the range and hitting-power of the
Western carrier strike forces. From the Russian
viewpoint in 1950, the foremost naval object-
lesson of World War II was not the commerce
destruction achieved by the German U-boat
force. It was, rather, the failure of the Japanese
submarine force to stop the US Navy's carriers
from ranging westward across the Pacific to the
doorstep of Japan.

The programme envisaged building 78 submarines a year, starting in 1950, to produce a
submarine force of 1200 boats by 1965. These
would then hold a triple defence line across the
sea approaches to the Soviet Union: 100 coastal
boats for the innermost zone, 900 medium-range

marines was high. Above all it was overtaken by the scorching progress made with Soviet nuclear research, which enabled the first Soviet submarine reactor to be put in hand as early as 1953, and the first nuclear submarine to enter service within a year of America's *Nautilus*.

When the original programme was scrapped after Stalin's death, only about one-third of the projected submarines ever entered the water. These, the first Soviet submarines built after World War II, owed much to the German Type VIIs and Type XXIs taken into service by the Soviet Navy after the war: diesel-electric types with streamlined hulls, fitted with bow and stern torpedo tubes and *schnorkel*. About 240 of the medium type—the 'Whiskey' class, as it is known in Western nomenclature—were built between 1951 and 1957, and 25 'Zulus', the latter ocean-going submarines. The Russians originally hoped to power the 'Zulu' submarines with an improved model of the Walter turbine, but they had no better luck than the British with this power plant and eventually substituted the conventional diesel-electric system. The 'Whiskeys' and 'Zulus' were followed with impressive speed by the first Soviet nuclear submarine: the 'November' class, introduced in 1958. It was armed with bow and stern torpedo tubes and was reported as having a surface speed of 20 knots, a submerged speed of 25 knots, and a diving capacity of 1650 feet.

Thirteen years after World War II, therefore, the submarine had virtually emerged as an entirely new weapon. Nuclear power enabled it to stay submerged on patrols of great duration, while inertial navigation guided it beneath the world's oceans, including the Arctic ice pack, with pinpoint accuracy. Now commerce destruction almost appeared as the least of roles for the most advanced submarines, like harnessing a racehorse to a farm cart. The future seemed to lie with the high-speed attack submarine, and with the hunter-killer seeking its prey in the depths. But those 13 years had also seen the American monopolies of nuclear weapons and nuclear submarines energetically broken by the Soviet Union. The nuclear arms race was on, and with it the search for the most effective— and unanswerable—delivery systems for nuclear weapons. As that search intensified in the late 1950s the submarine, with its capacious hull, was now pressed into service in its most awesome role: as the unseen vehicle for the 'ultimate deterrent'.

boats for the central zone and 200 long-range, ocean-going boats for the outer zone. This scheme contained a host of errors. It was an attempt to apply land strategy to the fluid problems of naval defence—a naval version of the zoned defences with which the Red Army had broken the last German summer offensive at Kursk in 1943, counterattacking to seize the initiative on the Eastern Front for good. It was a strategic misuse of the submarine, requiring an essentially offensive weapon to be used defensively. It was a dangerously restrictive programme because such a commitment took no account of the constant improvements being made to submarines at the time, and the danger of ending up with a vast fleet of obsolete sub-

Attack submarine USS *Barb* at sea, December 1973.

The towering, streamlined 'sail' of USS *Finback*, *Sturgeon* class attack submarine.

Through the Arctic ice. Top: USS *Whale* surfaces at the North Pole, 6 April 1969. Above: USS *Trepang* breaks surface during exercise 'Wepex '71', January 1971.

# 7. THE DOOMSDAY SHIPS

138/

In military terms a country does not become a nuclear power just because it learns how to make a nuclear explosion. To guarantee full membership in what has been called the 'nuclear club', an 'independent delivery system'—independent, that is to say, of political control by another power—is essential. This delivery system can be of several types. The simplest of all is that used for small 'tactical' nuclear weapons for battlefield use: packing the nuclear device into the warhead of a shell and firing it out of a long-range gun. In 1945 Hiroshima and Nagasaki were destroyed by high-flying B29 bombers attacking in conventional style: flying directly over the target and dropping the bomb with parachutes, with a time fuse to explode it in the air over the target. But this had only proved possible because the Japanese no longer controlled their own air-space—they had no fighters capable of intercepting the B29s or anti-aircraft missiles capable of shooting them down. It was this danger that led to the adoption of remote-controlled missiles for the delivery of nuclear weapons, and the 1950s were the years of their begetting.

The latter years of World War II had seen a growing range of missiles used to deliver high-explosive warheads to their targets. After the war cryptic sets of initials, describing basic missile function, helped proliferate the nightmare jargon of modern warfare:

SAM—Surface-to-Air Missile
AAM—Air-to-Air Missile
ASM—Air-to-Surface Missile
SSM—Surface-to-Surface Missile

Nearly all the first missiles used in combat were short-range, solid-fuel missiles with no guidance systems, but by the end of the war the first guided missiles had been introduced. These were ASMs dropped from a parent aircraft and guided to their target by radio control, the latter being operated from the aircraft. This was the first

system used to relieve bombers of the need actually to fly over the target in order to drop nuclear bombs—the 'stand-off' bomb, dropped from outside the enemy's AA gun and SAM defences and guided to the target under its own power.

In the early 1950s, however, the Americans and Soviets were pushing ahead with experiments in improving Germany's wartime 'V-weapons'. Two of these, totally different in type, had been used in the last year of the war, and both had proved capable of bombing London from the Continent. The first was the V1, a pilotless aircraft with stub wings—the first CM, or cruise missile. It flew on a pulse-jet engine and was just slow enough to be intercepted by the fastest piston-engined aircraft of the day, or shot down by barrage AA gunfire. But the V2 rocket, plunging down onto its target from its lofty flight trajectory through the stratosphere, was a totally different proposition. It could not be shot down or diverted in flight. It could be fired hundreds of miles from the target with no danger to a human crew. Here was the ideal vehicle for nuclear warheads, once sufficiently accurate guidance systems had been

Previous pages: Superb bows-on shot of *Resolution*, Britain's first ballistic missile submarine. Above: Wartime pioneer of Polaris —test-firing of *pulver-raketen* from a submerged Type IX U-boat, summer 1942. *Right*: USS *Grayback*, designed to carry the Regulus cruise missile.

Below: With the Polaris era only months away, USS *Halibut* test-fires a Regulus on 31 March 1960.

added to make sure of hitting the target, and sufficiently powerful rockets developed to make sure of reaching the target. This was the dreaded ICBM—Inter-Continental Ballistic Missile—which was added to the rival nuclear armouries in the late 1950s.

The trouble with the ICBM, however, was that it had to be fired from a 'fixed address'; it was too big to be moved around on mobile launching-platforms of the type used for the V2 at the end of the war. Once the ICBMs' launching site had been pinpointed by enemy reconnaissance it would naturally become the first target for the enemy's ICBMs. This led to two developments: the move towards 'second-level deterrence' (the ability to launch a second nuclear strike after the first one had brought down the enemy's retaliatory strike); and the frantic search for an effective Submarine-Launched Ballistic Missile (SLBM) which could be fired from any point within the enormous radius of a nuclear submarine.

As the Germans had found in the war, the cruise missile was the easier type to develop and by 1955 the American and Soviet Navies were both working on adapting the cruise missile for firing from submarines; it was referred to as the SLCM, or Sea-Launched Cruise Missile. The problems of the SLCM were twofold. First, the parent submarine had to approach dangerously close to the enemy's coastline; second, the missile had to be launched on the surface. The leading American cruise missile of the middle and late 1950s was the Regulus, and for a while continuing setbacks to the US long-range rocket programme brought Regulus to the fore as the only strategic nuclear missile capable of being launched from a submarine. In February 1956 the Americans announced that *Grayback* and *Growler*, originally laid down as diesel-electric attack submarines, were to be completed as guided-missile submarines for the deployment of Regulus. The two submarines were cut in two and cylindrical hangars installed above the bows to carry the missiles. Automatic loading and firing gear enabled the submarine to surface, extract a Regulus from the hangar straight onto an inclined built-in launch ramp, fire the missile and submerge at once.

*Grayback* and *Growler* became operational in 1958 and within a year the Soviet Navy had countered with an equivalent stop-gap: the 'Whiskey Twin-Cylinder' conversion. Much clumsier than the built-in hangars used in *Grayback* and *Growler*, the 'Whiskey Twin-Cylinder' was, as its name suggests, a 'Whiskey' class boat with a couple of cylindrical missile hangars fitted aft of the sail. It gave the Soviets much-needed test experience with their new cruise missile, the SS-N-3 'Shaddock'. But it was, to quote *Jane's Fighting Ships*, 'Probably never truly operational, being a thoroughly messy conversion which must make a noise like a train if proceeding at any speed above dead slow when dived'.

For the American submarine fleet, however, the *Grayback* and *Growler* conversions proved to be no more than stop-gaps. After a traumatic three years in which it had seemed that the Soviet Union was well on the way to establishing a decisive lead over the United States in long-range rocketry, the Americans dramatically unveiled their Polaris programme and the giant new ships which would carry it.

By the second half of the 1950s the United States and the Soviet Union were working on the problem of launching the first orbiting satellite around the Earth. International prestige was the least of the prizes at stake. Orbiting satellites would transform global weather forecasting, electronic communications, and the gathering of astronomical data outside the murk of the Earth's atmosphere. They would also open a new era in both military and naval reconnaissance, surveillance, and as likely as not missile control and delivery from space. The result was a bizarre symbiosis between the nuclear arms race and space exploration: the techniques of mass destruction and the most inspiring challenge ever taken up by the human race paradoxically feeding off each other. And the powerful new rockets, improved control and communication needed to launch and recover spacecraft resulted in an ever-deadlier array of nuclear weaponry.

As the world knows, the Soviets were first into space, launching Sputnik 1 on 4 October 1957 and following it with Sputnik 2, carrying the dog, Laika, on 3 November. The immediate American reaction, from an understandable state of shock, was to risk and reap humiliating failure by unsuccessfully trying to launch the

US Navy Vanguard satellite with maximum publicity. When Vanguard blew up on the launch pad on 6 December 1957, watched by a television audience of millions, credibility in the much-vaunted American technological superiority could hardly have received a more drastic shaking. Some of this credibility was restored on 31 January 1958 when the US Army's Explorer 1 satellite was launched, followed at last by Vanguard 1 on 17 March; but the Soviets countered on 15 May by launching Sputnik 3, weighing nearly 3000 pounds. The 31 pounds of Explorer and the three-pound Vanguard— scorned by Soviet Premier Nikita Krushchev as the 'Grapefruit'—caused deepening dismay when nuclear payloads were mentally substituted.

With the big Russian rockets grabbing the headlines in 1957–58, it was not easy to see how their supremacy had come about, or how temporary a phenomenon it was. The Americans had not rushed ahead with long-range rocket development after 1945 because they did not have to. They had the world's biggest strategic bombing force and carrier fleet already on hand for the long- and medium-range delivery of nuclear weapons. But Soviet rocket development, so triumphantly demonstrated with the first space shots, had been intended to cancel out and surpass American air supremacy. It enabled the Soviet Union to launch the first orbital satellites and manned spacecraft between 1957 and 1961—but this in turn prodded the Americans into developing their more sophisticated Atlas and Titan ICBMs for their Mercury and Gemini space programmes. By 1966 the United States had 904 ICBMs to the Soviet Union's 292.

With nuclear weapons as with the space programme, the Soviet rocket lead proved as superficial as it was temporary. The Russian obsession with developing heavy liquid-fuel rocket boosters for launching from land sites led to neglect of smaller solid-fuel rockets less suited to carrying the bulkier, cruder payloads created by Soviet technology. The Americans, on the other hand, while apparently completely outclassed by the feats of Soviet rocketry, were able to apply their superior technology and adopt solid-fuel missiles as a highly sophisticated nuclear delivery system. And these missiles, unlike the heavyweights with which Krushchev's USSR was making so much spectacular play, were sufficiently economical in size to be mounted in nuclear submarines.

The result was Polaris.

The Polaris formula took the streamlined, teardrop submarine hull of the *Skipjack* class—none of which had even been launched when Sputnik 1 went up—and stretched it by a breathtaking 130 feet, from 251 to 381 feet in overall length. The huge hull volume thus created was used to accommodate two rows of eight vertical rocket-launching tubes abaft the fin. Each of these 16 missiles could be assigned a different target and all were designed for underwater launching, the rocket engine cutting in as the missile broke surface and the guidance system correcting the missile's attitude to provide the correct flight trajectory to the target. And the real versatility of the Polaris formula was—and remains—immunity from retaliation by enemy land-based missiles, plus the unlimited initial radius provided by the submarine's nuclear power plant before a single missile is even fired.

The decision to introduce Polaris was taken while the United States was still being rocked by sputnik mania in the winter of 1957–58. Three new submarines specifically designed for carry-carrying Polaris were ordered in the Supplemental New Construction Programme signed on 11 February 1958. Two more were ordered in July 1958. The lead ship of the class, *George Washington*, was launched on 9 June 1959 and commissioned on 15 November of that year. And on 20 July 1960, lying submerged off the Florida coast, she made the first successful firing of the new weapon. Two missiles were launched, their performance being carefully monitored from the nearby 'spaceport' on Cape Canaveral. The test was successful: the Polaris era had arrived. Two years later the Polaris system was given its first complete test, from underwater firing to warhead detonation. This happened on 6 May 1962 when *Ethan Allen*, first of the second batch of five Polaris submarines laid down between 1959 and 1961, fired a Polaris A-2 in the Pacific Test Area of Christmas Island.

With the Polaris concept, the role of the submarine as an instrument of undersea war changed completely. There were no precedents for this change, nor any convenient parallel case-histories of land, air or sea weaponry to make the change any easier to describe. The 'Strategic Ballistic Missile Submarine' or SSBN did not render all other types of nuclear and diesel-electric submarines obsolete. On the contrary, these continue to be built and introduced to service as a vital element of conventional naval deployment, supplementary to the posture of strategic deterrence. But the Polaris SSBN was the first warship deliberately designed to threaten the destruction of 16 enemy cities with their civilian populations. And the grim novelty of this role makes it impossible to consider the SSBN in the context of conventional undersea war.

When taken as an abstract, the SSBN is an object of despair to anyone inclined to disenchantment with the human condition. Here is the distillation of human knowledge and ingenuity in an ultra-sophisticated weapon of mass destruction. It is intended to help save the world from nuclear warfare by making its own use unthinkable, and yet its possible use as the result of human error or failure cannot be

dismissed. Small wonder that objectors to the immorality and waste of nuclear weapons choose to focus their outrage on the SSBN as the deadliest and most insane menace of them all. And yet, given the destructive potential of nuclear weapons, it is still possible to look back over the first 20 years of the SSBN's existence and claim that it has not done badly as a deterrent. At the time of writing, we have managed to get through 35 years since the first puny atomic bombs were used on flesh and blood over Hiroshima and Nagasaki. During those 35 years, nuclear and thermonuclear weapons of far greater destructiveness have been contrived and brought to operational readiness—but none of them has been used, either by accident or design. The rulers of the superpowers have become adept in the art of crisis management in a crisis-ridden three and a half decades, which in a non-nuclear environment must surely have resulted in a Third World War. And 20 of those 35 years have been the years of the SSBN.

The advent of Polaris and its manifest advantages caused extensive restructuring of nuclear deterrent forces, both inside the United States and among her NATO allies. As more and more American SSBNs came into service through the 1960s and the stockpile of nuclear warheads grew, the former importance of strategic bombing forces began to recede. For example the total of American strategic bombers dropped from 630 in 1966 to 373 in 1977. After a costly flirtation with the American Skybolt stand-off bomb, Britain, in 1962, decided to wind down her strategic bombing force and adopt Polaris herself, building her own

With the French strategic nuclear fleet. Below: Testing the manual firing controls in the 'forest' of *Redoutable*'s launching-tubes. Below right: Loading an MSBS M-20 into one of the tubes. Opposite: France's SLBM, the MSBS M-1.

submarines but taking the American missile. The four ships of the *Resolution* class were laid down in 1964–65; *Resolution*, the first into service, was commissioned in October 1967. France followed suit with her *Redoutable* class, the first of which *Redoutable*, became operational in December 1971. Unlike Britain, France elected to develop her own missile 'family'. (Considerably advanced in rocket development over her European neighbours, the French joined the ranks of the space powers by putting their first satellite into orbit in November 1965, launched from a French-made Diamant rocket.) France went on to fit her SSBN fleet with her own ballistic missile, the MSBS.

In retrospect, one of the most intriguing points about the adoption of the SSBN is that it took place during the last 15 years of world affluence, 1958–73, before the Yom Kippur War in the Middle East and the ensuing world energy and economic crisis—for the financial cost was appalling. *Skipjack* had cost $40 million; *Ethan Allen* cost $105 million. As for the main American SSBN fleet of no less than 31 ships (*Lafayette* and *Benjamin Franklin* classes, laid down between January 1961 and March 1965) they cost about $109.5 million *each*. However, these were only the construction costs; on top of the amounts mentioned above one must add the cost of replacing nuclear cores (about $3.5 million apiece) and repeatedly up-dating the ballistic missiles as bigger and better models are developed. Quite apart from their SSBN programme, the Americans were proceeding with their huge nuclear-powered aircraft-carriers of the *Enterprise* and *Nimitz* classes, the biggest floating structures ever built. *Enterprise*, commissioned in 1961, cost $451.3 million; but the many delays to her successor, *Nimitz*, not commissioned until May 1975, increased its cost to $1.881 *billion*. And the combined defence appropriations for the American SSBN and nuclear carrier construction programmes were nothing to the $40 billion set aside for the Apollo

Opposite: British SSBN HMS *Revenge* at speed.

moon programme before the United States had succeeded in putting so much as a mouse into Earth orbit.

The decision of Britain to adopt Polaris deserves special comment. It was prompted by the obvious political conviction that the country should retain an independent nuclear deterrent. Given the fact that there were no conceivable circumstances under which Britain could find herself facing a nuclear conflict with the United States, and given the enormous destructive potential of the American SSBN fleet, it is highly questionable whether Britain's ability to keep two SSBNs constantly at sea (and she has not always managed to do even that) acts as a genuinely independent deterrent on the Soviet Union. Britain's increasing economic problems over the past 20 years, even with the safety-net of North Sea Oil, make the high cost of the British SSBN force seem an excessive price to pay for a nominally independent deterrent. (*Resolution* cost £40.24 million without her missiles, while the combined cost of *Repulse*, *Resolution* and *Revenge* was £116.05 million.)

Britain was, moreover, faced in the 1960s with a familiar menace which, after her traumatic experiences in the two World Wars, she should have been the first to diagnose. This was the rapid naval growth of a potentially hostile nation with submarine development in the forefront of its naval priorities. Between 1958 and 1968, the Soviet Union advanced from 21st to 5th place among the maritime nations of the world. In terms of economic vulnerability nothing has changed for Britain since World War II: her livelihood remains totally dependent on seaborne imports which have to be paid for with seaborne exports (in Britain's case with increasing lack of success). While nuclear devastation remains a nightmare possibility, starvation by sea inflicted by enemy submarines

Below: The Navigator at work in the control room of HMS *Repulse*.

Left: USS *Whale* surfaced at the North Pole April 1969. Below: HMS *Resolution*'s galley. Bottom: A far cry from the cramped confines of the pioneering days—the helmsmen's positions in *Redoutable*. Right: The endless round of checks and tests. The Assistant Polaris Systems Officer-in-Charge at a monitoring panel in *Resolution*.

has twice provided a harrowing case-history in how Britain can be brought to the brink of defeat by conventional naval forces.

With the British Isles straddling the Soviet Union's naval exit-routes into the Atlantic, the money devoured by the SSBN force could have been spent to no less effect, and probably far better, on making it demonstrably impossible for Soviet submarines to operate in the North Atlantic without Britain's toleration. If Britain could hardly be expected to match the Americans ship for ship, building enough nuclear hunter-killer submarines to cope with a mass attack on the North Atlantic sealane by Russian submarines, she could certainly have built the strongest surface force in the Western alliance and contented herself with the main anti-submarine role.

Having elected to join the SSBN nuclear deterrers, however, Britain could certainly not afford to keep pace with the high-speed development of SLBM missiles. The original Polaris A-1 missile had a range of 1200 nautical miles. This was almost immediately improved by Polaris

Above: *Lafayette*, first of the US Navy's '3rd generation' Polaris submarines, is launched at Groton in 1962. Left: *Lafayette* class USS *Daniel Boone* at sea. Opposite, top: the 'forest' of launching-tubes in USS *John Adams*. Opposite, centre: Sonar watch in USS *Ulysses S. Grant*. Right: Commander of *Ulysses S. Grant* at the periscope, in a control room whose size and cleanliness few old-time submariners would have found credible. Far right: USS *James Madison* bids farewell to one of her Polaris tubes in 1969, scheduled for replacement with Poseidon.

A-2 with 1500 miles, and in October 1963 the *Andrew Jackson* fired the first Polaris A-3 off Cape Canaveral. Polaris A-3 not only had a vastly improved range of 2500 miles but it also delivered a cluster of three separate nuclear warheads to the same target. This 'parcelling' of nuclear warheads ushered in the second generation of submarine-launched ballistic missiles ponderously initialled as MIRV: 'Multiple Independently-targetable Re-entry Vehicle'. In the case of Poseidon, the first SLBM MIRVed missile and successor to Polaris A-3, this meant a missile which, like Polaris, can be carried by a SSBN and launched from under water with a range of 2500 miles. But once in flight its payload splits into ten mini-missiles, each capable of being steered to a separate target. Thus instead of being able to hit 16 enemy targets, as with Polaris, a SSBN armed with Poseidon can hit 160. The ten *George Washington*s and *Ethan Allen*s of the SSBN 'first generation' were not suitable for conversion to Poseidon, but by 1978 all 31 of the *Lafayette*s and *Benjamin Franklin*s had been fitted with Poseidon. With

Polaris A-3 (left) compared with the larger, MIRVed Poseidon.

the Polaris missiles of the earlier SSBNs the overall American SSBN fleet was now able to fire a combined theoretical total (theoretical, because not all the ships are simultaneously at sea) of 5020 nuclear warheads—55 percent of the total United States nuclear deterrent.

But Poseidon was not to be the last word. In 1976 the Americans laid down the first of the giant (18,000 tons) *Ohio* class SSBNs. *Ohio*, first of the class, was launched in November 1978. She carries no less than 24 launching-tubes for

First successful launch of Trident, 8 June 1979.

the 'third-generation' SLBM, Trident, with MIRVed warhead and a nominal range of 4000 miles. *Michigan*, second of the class, approaches completion at the time of writing. It was hard to see the SSBN being evolved much further until, in mid-November 1980, the Soviet Union launched the first of her 'Typhoon' class giants. At 30,000 tons they are far bigger than many NATO aircraft-carriers, and though their 20 SS-N-18 SLBMs are believed not to be MIRVed they out-range Trident by 1200 miles.

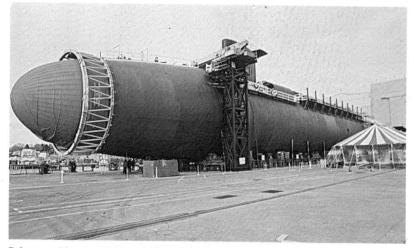

Colossus—*Ohio* class Trident SSBN, USS *Michigan*, at Groton in April 1979.

First of the Trident giants: USS *Ohio* in the water, with the towering bulk of *Michigan* at left.

Caught completely on the wrong foot by the early American commitment to the SSBN, the Soviet Union spent a desperate decade of improvisation and experiment to develop an equivalent system. The first Russian method used for firing missiles from submarines (apart from cruise missiles employed in the long-range SSM role) consisted of lengthening the sail to produce a streamlined fairing capable of carrying ballistic missiles in two or three vertically mounted tubes. This process, begun as early as 1955 with converted 'Zulu' class boats, actually made the Soviet Union the first sea power to produce a ballistic missile submarine. But the

only Russian missile small enough to be carried in a submarine was the tiny 'Sark' with a range of no more than 300 miles, and by the late 1950s it was not to be expected that any diesel-electric submarine would be able to get within 300 miles of the American continent without being detected.

Nevertheless, this was the system with which the Russians proceeded into the 1960s, building small successive batches of submarines capable of carrying missiles of increasing range. The 'Golf' variants, 21 in all, were accompanied by the 13 'Hotel' class, appearing between 1958 and 1962; both were originally equipped with

'Sark', but subsequently equipped with the SS-N-5 'Serb', with a range of 700 miles. Experience thus gained led to the USSR's answer to the American Polaris SSBN: the 8500-ton 'Yankee' class, which appeared in 1967. The 'Yankee' SSBN imitated the whale-shaped, elongated hull of the American boats and also mounted its missiles in 16 vertical tubes—but the range of its SSN-6 'Sawfly' missiles was only 1300 miles, and even when improved in later marks this range still fell far short of the 2500 miles of Polaris A-3 and Poseidon.

The 1970s have seen the Soviet Union doggedly catching up with the enormous lead established by the American SSBN force in the 1960s. The 'Delta' class SS-N-18 missile took the Soviet SSBN force through the 5000-mile range barrier, and the first Soviet experiments with MIRVing were soon detected. In 1976, the first year in which comparisons in MIRVed warheads could be drawn, the Soviet Union was estimated to have only 140 missiles to the American 1046—or 2970 independently-targetable warheads (ICBMs and SLBMs combined) to the American 7274. By 1976 the Russians had produced the 'Delta III', armed with the SS-N-18 of no less than 5200 miles' range—capable of hitting any part of the northern hemisphere from Soviet-controlled waters. Soviet MIRVing continues to improve at the time of writing, and the likelihood of the Soviet Union achieving MIRV parity in the near future can be no more than delayed by the American Trident programme. The newest, 30,000-ton 'Typhoons' are also designed for the SS-N-18, but will almost certainly be used as test-beds for more sophisticated MIRVed Soviet SLBMs in the near future.

No class of warship other than the ballistic missile submarine has ever been able to unleash catastrophe upon the world—yet with each year that passes without nuclear war, the doomsday ships will continue to do their job. Lord Fisher's prophecy, back in 1904, of the 'immense impending revolution which the submarines will effect as offensive weapons of war', has been awesomely fulfilled. And it was also Fisher who had shocked the Hague Peace Conference of 1899 by asserting that 'War should be terrible! You may as well talk of civilizing Hell!' Like the great battleships which Fisher created, swinging idly round their anchors through nearly all of World War I, the merciful inactivity of the nuclear doomsday ships can hardly be considered a failure when the alternative is too horrible to contemplate.

Opposite, top: Soviet 'Zulu V' experimental boat: two ballistic missiles mounted in the sail of an otherwise conventional diesel-electric submarine, as spotted by air air reconnaissance in November 1970. Below: Soviet 'Yankee' class ballistic missile submarine, armed—like its American, British and French counterparts—with 16 launch tubes aft of the sail (August 1976).

# 8. TECHNIQUES OF SURVEILANCE, 1945 - 80

156/

With submarines that could cruise further, submarines that could go faster, and submarines that could dive deeper, the techniques of submarine detection and destruction current at the end of World War II were bound to undergo an equally profound change as that wrought by the advent of the all-submerged nuclear submarine.

One of the biggest ironies of the story of submarine detection has been the resurrection of the hydrophone, established as virtually useless in World War I. Of the four major techniques used to detect submarines, sound detection plays its part in two of them. This is carried out either by sonobuoy dropped from aircraft and left to listen—the method first introduced at the end of World War II—or by permanent listening-posts positioned on the continental shelfs. For even the most streamlined submarine, moving at speed through the water, emits a distinctive sound-pattern which can be analysed to identify the type and speed—and hence the weaponry—of the target.

Apart from this static listening technique, there is the method made possible by the development of the naval, shipborne helicopter in the 1950s. This method is known as 'dunking', and in anything but impossible flying weather guarantees the ship which launches the helicopter constant surveillance. Flying low over the water, the helicopter 'dunks' its payload beneath the surface, and if it hears nothing

moves to another area and searches there.

Sound detection, however, only provides a useful crosscheck to sonar, which is still the main detection-system carried not only in surface warships alone, but in submarines, by 'dunking' helicopters, and by towed surface arrays. Thus the submarine at large beneath the high seas, operating in predictable patrol areas, can now be located by sound or sonar from five different directions at once: from seabed listening-posts, from 'dunking' helicopters, from surface warships, from other submarines, and from air-dropped sonobuoys.

Previous pages: A Grumman S-2E Tracker, its MAD gear extended, flies over a schnorkelling submarine off the Californian coast. Above and below: *Plus ça change, plus c'est la même chose—* Coastal 'blimp' and Q-ship, 1917; RAF Nimrod and patrolling submarines, 1969. Opposite, top: Listening equipment in the sound room aboard HMS *Resolution*, 1974. Right: US Navy underwater sonar array is raised to the surface.

All this versatility in sound and sonar detection, however, would be of little practical use without the revolution in communications which the computer and space age has brought in its train. Since 1945 systems have been brought into existence—and are still being planned and improved—which enable ships at sea to be passed instant information on both enemy and friendly submarine deployment. These systems connect the commands of fleets at sea with co-ordinating fleet command centres ashore, and also with the emergency flying communications headquarters which exercise 'C3'—Command, Control and Communications—from the air.

For obvious reasons, data are only available for the NATO line-up, but in outline it works as follows. The Fleet Command Centre (FCC) processes and displays information for the Fleet Commander-in-Chief, American National Command Authorities and Navy Department, and constantly exchanges information with the tactical commanders afloat. The latter, in their Tactical Flag Command Centres, give each flag commander an up-to-date situation display, enabling him to plan and direct operations. And the provision of all relevant information to make this comprehensive hook-up work is the

The meshing techniques of undersea surveillance being used simultaneously by the Soviet Union and Western powers today.
*Ocean bed.* (1) Chains of hydrophones—'ours' and 'theirs'—listen for missile-firing submarines (2) and attack submarines (3) which are also listening for each other.
*Edge of continental shelf.* (4) Fixed long-range sonar array.
*Surface.* (5) Anti-submarine surface warships; (6) Static buoys; (7) Helicopters 'dunking' sonar buoys (8).
*Air.* (9) Medium-range and (10, 11) long-range anti-submarine aircraft, dropping sonar buoys. (12) Barra-type buoy dropped from aircraft, lowering its sonar head beneath confusing thermal water layers near surface.
*Space.* (13) Orbiting satellites, co-ordinating the hunt and speeding the flow of data between shore and seagoing commands.

Top: American P-3 Orions patrolling off the Vietnamese coast, October 1966. Above: RAF Nimrod over the Soviet helicopter-carrier *Moskva* in 1974.

role of the Ocean Surveillance Information System—OSIS.

None of this would be possible without computer-processed information—'sound libraries' of the characteristics of leading ship types, plus 'radar and electronic libraries' containing similar known characteristics. A hydrophone or seabed listening-post locates a distant submarine; automatic computer comparison checks out the information and reports a 'Whiskey Twin-Cylinder' submarine proceeding submerged at ten knots, and so on. This information is instantaneously flashed to the nearest NATO flag commander for appropriate action, and simultaneously displayed ashore on all major co-ordinating display boards.

More and more data input equipment con-

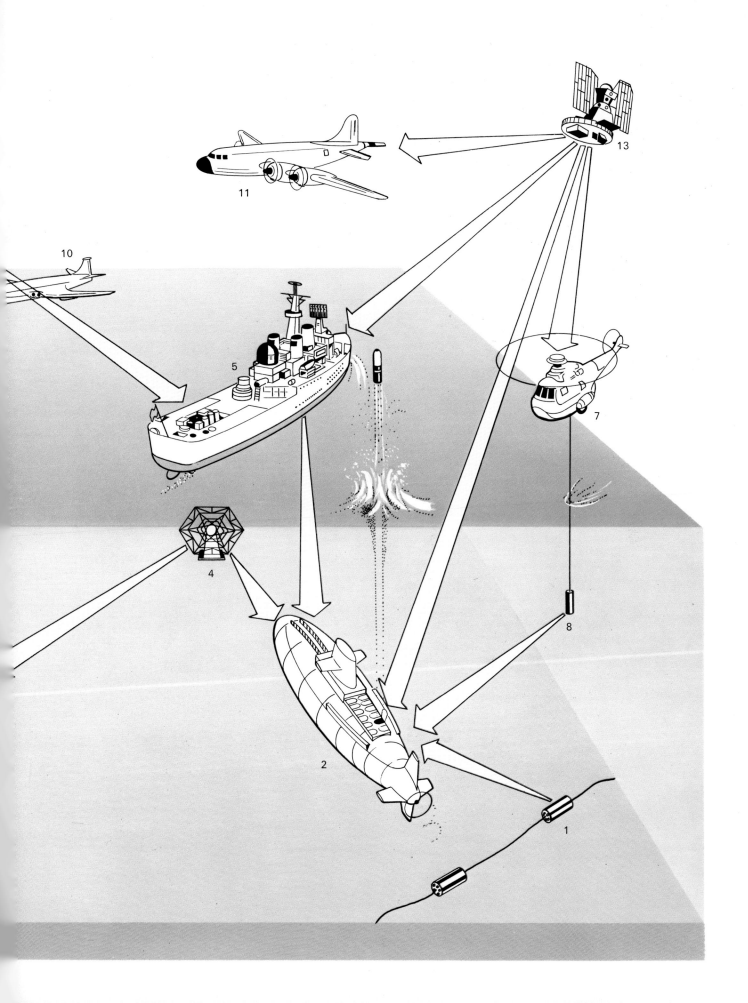

Right: An 'all-in-one' demonstration of anti-submarine warfare techniques 20 years ago (June 1960). 'Dunking' helicopter at right, conventional submarines USS *Darter* and *Chopper*, anti-submarine destroyers USS *Calcaterra* and *Hazelwood*, with S2F and P2V detection and attack aircraft overhead. Inset, below: A Sea King helicopter from HMS *Ark Royal* 'dunks' a sonobuoy.

tinues to be added to the system, forming component sub-systems of great complexity. An excellent example is the US Navy's ASWCCCS—'Anti-Submarine Warfare Centre Command and Control System', worldwide in scope. This is fed by two main sources of information: sound detection from the seabed, and sound detection by towed surface arrays. The former, known as SOSUS—Sound Surveillance System—is made up of networks of seabed detector posts around the United States. The latter, operated from the surface, is SURTASS —Surveillance Towed Array Surveillance System. SURTASS consists of long arrays of passive sonar sensors, methodically towed at slow speed over integrated patrol lines. SUR-

Below: Depth-charge
dropped by an American
P-3 Orion.

TASS is one of the latest elements to be added
to the surveillance network, the first three
specialised ships for the programme being
ordered in the American 1978 defence budget.
The acoustic data thus gathered are flashed to
an Acoustic Research Centre (ARC) in California, where massed computer power goes to
work on even the weakest acoustic sounds
emitted by submarines over long ranges.

Apart from the obvious use of reconnaissance
satellites to monitor submarines proceeding on
the surface, satellite communications are vital
to speed the flow of information, as with the
transfer of SURTASS information from the
parent ships to the California ARC. Security is
provided by the device known as 'packet-
switching'. A message can be broken down into
a thousand or more fragments or 'packets'.
Each packet contains a coded address of the
message's intended recipient, and the trans-
mitting computer automatically routes the
packets over any free route in the communications network. On arrival, the packets are
reassembled by computer and an acknowledge-
ment flashed back to the sender.

On a gigantic scale, all this computer wizardry
repeats the communications breakthrough
achieved in World War II by the TBS radio
telephone, which for the first time enabled the

The mine—as potent a weapon of undersea war as ever. Top: Loading a dummy Mk 25 mine into a P-3 Orion. Above: A good old-fashioned anchored mine is dropped by a US fleet tug during exercises off the Philippines in January 1978.

Above: Soviet Il-38 'May' anti-submarine reconnaissance aircraft drops a sonobuoy during exercises in the North Atlantic in April 1975. Right: Cast in the role of submarine-hunter but packing a ferocious surface-to-surface armament as well is the *Minsk*, the second Soviet *Kiev* class carrier, with 'Forger' jump-jets and helicopters (February 1979). Far right, top: Icelandic coastguard personnel survey a Soviet undersea listening device retrieved off Iceland in the early 1970s. Beneath the outer casing were found 32 hydrophones.

commanders of task forces and hunting groups to direct operations by voice instead of laboriously flashing a visual or radio morse signal. What is new, however, is the global scope of the system and the virtual achievement of 'real time' in the passing and analysis of surveillance data. NATO believes that its submarine surveillance network, as with its weaponry, is superior to the Soviet and Warsaw Pact equivalent. But it also knows from painful experience that the Soviet story is one of constant improvement.

Another direct link with the early days of World War I is known today as ECM—Electronic Counter-Measures. This involves nothing more or less than trying to jam the enemy's equipment and confuse him.

One of the greatest problems has yet to be solved: shore-to-ship communication with submerged submarines, the value of which with regard to the SSBN force is obvious. This has been partially solved by VLF (Very Low Frequency) wavelengths, which can penetrate sea water to a certain extent; but the real obstacle is that of communicating with a submarine several hundred feet below the surface. One hopeful solution is ELF (Extra Low Frequency) transmission; but the huge size of the ELF transmitters required for use on a global scale has run into inevitable heated opposition on environmental grounds.

The last vital legacy of World War II submarine detection, the Magnetic Anomaly Detector, still plays a vital role. It is used by surveillance aircraft on ocean patrols and is particularly valuable for detecting submarines which surface and try to camouflage themselves in the Arctic pack.

# 9. BALANCE SHEET, 1980

Previous pages: The
watchers—Task Force 60,
US 6th Fleet, in the
Mediterranean (March
1976). Below: Soviet
'Victor' class nuclear fleet
submarine, South China
Sea, April 1974. Opposite:
Soviet 'Juliet' class cruise
missile submarine.

Having traced the major milestones in submarine development since World War II and
examined the most significant changes in technology and weaponry, it is time to assemble
these components and see how the balance
stands in the only full-scale naval confrontation
which a Third World War is likely to produce.
This confrontation would pit the Soviet Russian
and Warsaw Pact Navies against the combined
fleets of NATO.

From NATO's point of view the immediate
future is black.

What has happened is that over the past 20
years the leading NATO powers—and especially
Britain—have become mesmerised by the ever-
increasing growth of NATO's strategic nuclear

potential. As this is the most costly military and
naval investment that a modern power can
make, economies have been enforced elsewhere,
at the expense of conventional land, sea and air
deployment. This has been accompanied by
repeated boasting about NATO's superiority
both in nuclear strike capacity and in conventional weapon quality. Such boasts have not
been accompanied by measures to cancel the
Soviet Union's sustained improvements to its
own nuclear and conventional defences.

NATO's peril lies in the formidable additions
which the Soviet Union and Warsaw Pact
countries have lavished upon their conventional
as well as nuclear forces, while the NATO
countries have been running down their own

conventional strength. In 1980 the balance in favour of Soviet and Warsaw Pact conventional land, sea and air forces is so strong that they could launch an overwhelming offensive *without* using nuclear weapons. For the past decade, NATO commanders in Europe have admitted that if so attacked, without the advance warning of deteriorating East/West relations which NATO strategy fondly imagines it will be granted in order to mobilise and reinforce before the attack, the frontline NATO forces would be overwhelmed in a matter of days.

To play its part in meeting and repelling such a conventional attack, the NATO Navies have two functions: to support the NATO ground forces in the Mediterranean and Scandinavia, and to prevent the Soviet Navy from gaining command of the North Atlantic sealane to Britain and the European Continent.

The NATO Navies, however, have become so depleted over the past 20 years that they are no longer capable of fulfilling both functions.

'Meanwhile,' comments Vice-Admiral Sir James Jungius in the *NATO Review* for January 1980, 'Soviet sea power has reached a level where it is capable of posing a serious threat in both areas simultaneously.' He quotes a NATO naval decline of some 27 percent for the period 1960–80, as set against a Soviet decline of only about 3.75 percent. Commenting on the same phenomenon in the British *Daily Telegraph* of 22 January 1980, naval correspondent Desmond Wettern had this to say in amplification:

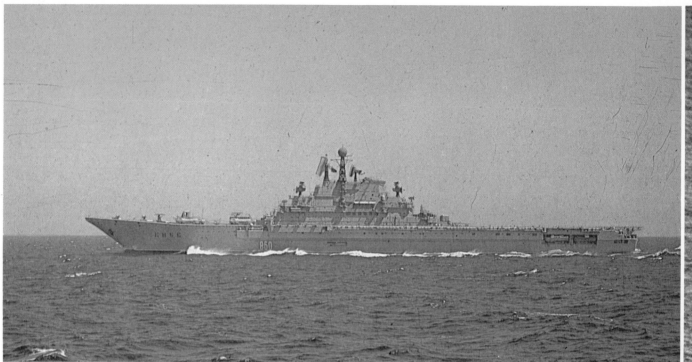

Left and below: *Kiev*'s first appearance in the Mediterranean, July 1976. Britain's decision to phase out carriers as 'outmoded' has been ominously replied to by the rapidly growing Soviet carrier fleet.

'In 1960 the Russian fleet included 28 cruisers, 154 destroyers, 77 frigates and 390 submarines, most of which were built during or even before the 1939–45 War, and their fighting value was doubtful.

Today, despite the introduction of so much more costly and effective missile-armed nuclear submarines, three aircraft-carriers with more building, and missile-armed surface ships, the number of submarines has dropped by only about 30 while, as in the Western navies, the total of destroyers has dropped by exactly half and the number of frigates has almost doubled.

In the Western navies there are some 250 submarines, not all of them in commission, and of these 122 are nuclear-powered compared with 156 in the Russian Navy . . .

*The two largest NATO navies, those of Britain and America, have suffered the heaviest reductions.*

*In June 1960 the Americans had some 817 warships and auxiliaries in commission, or almost exactly 300 more than today; while the Royal Navy had 205 ships including four carriers, five cruisers, 34 submarines and 84 destroyers and frigates compared with 144 in 1980, which includes two helicopter carriers but no cruisers; 23 submarines and 50 destroyers and frigates.'* [Author's italics]

In other words, the NATO Navies, should they decide to abandon the task of supporting the ground forces on the strategic flanks in the event of a Soviet assault, are woefully short of the surface escort and hunter-killer forces needed

172/

for keeping control of the North Atlantic. For NATO the biggest menace to the Atlantic sealane would come from the Soviet Navy's Northern Fleet, based at Kola Inlet on the Russian Murmansk coast and at Archangel on the White Sea. In the 1979–80 review of *The Military Balance* compiled by the London-based Institute for Strategic Studies, the Northern Fleet's strength was assessed at 120 submarines and 70 major surface combat ships.

To contain the Northern Fleet, NATO's primary deployment would be drawn from the American, Canadian and British Navies, which in the same review were assessed as having 157 major surface combat ships (including five American carriers) and 29 British and Canadian submarines. Assuming that 50 out of the 80 nuclear and diesel attack submarines would be deployed in the North Atlantic (no longer a warrantable assumption since the USSR's demonstration of her ability to operate carrier task forces on both sides of the world at once, in 1979) this would bring the NATO submarine strength up to 79.

Seventy-nine NATO submarines, not all fitted for hunter-killer work, would then be set against 120 Soviet submarines, which in turn, backed by their own 70 surface warships, would

be set against 157 NATO surface warships. NATO's supposed technological superiority would have to be miraculously high to overcome such odds, even allowing for the submarine-hunting capacity provided by the five American carriers. But in 1980 it is no longer clear how much longer this superiority can seriously be claimed.

'West Outclassed by Latest Soviet Submarines', warned the *Daily Telegraph* in Britain on 22 August 1979. 'Russia is now believed to have at sea four Alpha class torpedo-armed nuclear submarines whose diving depth and speed would enable them to evade most Western anti-submarine weapons. They can dive to depths of 3000 to 4000 feet, far greater than any Western nuclear submarines—the principal anti-submarine weapons—can attain. The underwater speed of the Russian submarines is known to be at least 40 knots, as the American Navy has been able to track them at such a speed on several occasions. . . . If the Alpha design were to be modified to carry anti-ship missiles, the task of protecting convoys would be immeasurably harder.'

Below: USS *Brooke* fires an ASROC anti-submarine missile. Right: Britain's first lightweight carrier, HMS *Invincible*. Her diminutive Twin Sea Dart launcher is perched in the bows beside the 'ski-jump' flare of the flight deck.

Nor can a NATO trouncing in a surface-to-surface clash be ruled out. Even *Kiev*, Russia's first anti-submarine aircraft carrier, which entered service in 1976, is equipped with four twin SS-N-12 surface-to-surface missile launchers, giving her a surface-to-surface fighting capacity of about 250 miles. By comparison HMS *Invincible*, Britain's newest anti-submarine carrier (or 'through-deck cruiser', as it is mendaciously known) is equipped with a solitary Twin Sea Dart launcher which must double as her SAM protection and has a range of only 40

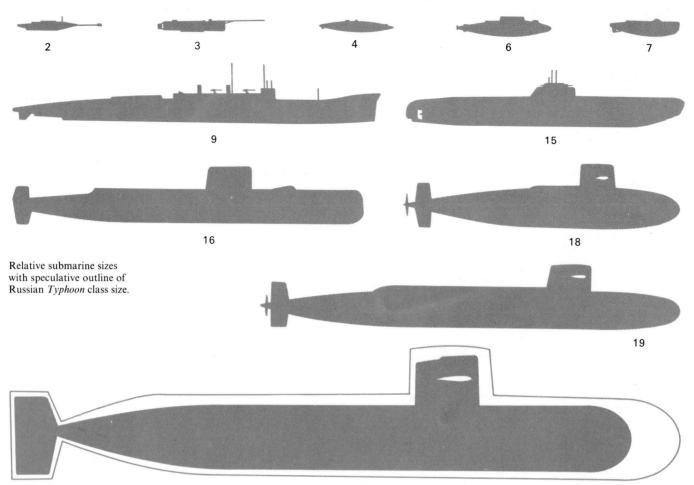

2      3      4      6      7

9                          15

16                         18

Relative submarine sizes
with speculative outline of
Russian *Typhoon* class size.

19

20

1. 1863 *Plongeur*. France.
First non-hand-driven
submarine, powered by
compressed air
2. 1863. *David* class. US
Steam-powered
3. 1864 *Hunley* class.
US Hand-cranked. First
to sink a warship
4. 1886 *Peral*. Spain.
First electric-battery-
powered submarine
5. 1888 *Gymnote*. France.
First submarine fitted with
self-propelled torpedoes
6. 1895 *Plunger*. US
Steam-powered on

surface; electric when
submerged
7. 1901 *Holland* class.
US designed
First submarine
commercially produced
in quantity
8. 1904 *Aigrette*. France.
First diesel-electric
submarine
9. 1917 'K' class. Britain.
Oil-fired steam turbines

gave fast surface speed
10. 1940 *Maiale* class.
Italy. Two-man chariot
with detachable warhead
11. 1940 *Kairyu* class.
Japan. Two-man midget
submarine
12. 1942 X-craft class.
Britain. Four-man midgets
13. 1943 *U-264*. Germany.
First operational U-boat;
fitted with a schnorkel

14. 1944 *U-791*. Germany.
Hydrogen peroxide used
as an experimental fuel
ingredient
15. 1944 Type XXI class
U-boats. Germany.
Streamlined hull and
more batteries used to
increase speed
16. 1955 *Nautilus*. US
First nuclear submarine
17. 1956 *Explorer*. Britain.

Hydrogen peroxide tested
as an alternative to
nuclear power
18. 1958 *Skipjack*. US
Pear-drop shaped hull
improved manoeuvra-
bility
19. *George Washington*
class. US First nuclear-
powered missile-firing
submarine
20. 1979. *Ohio* class. US

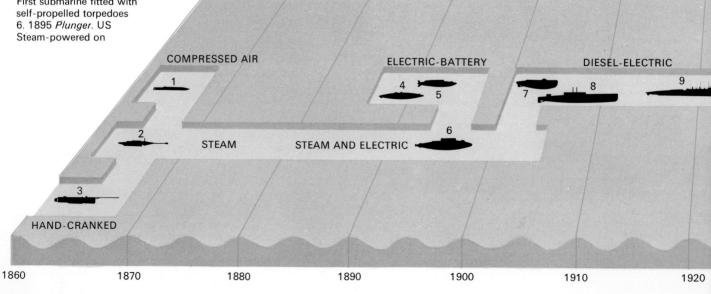

COMPRESSED AIR          ELECTRIC-BATTERY          DIESEL-ELECTRIC

1                    4      5              7      8              9

2          STEAM          STEAM AND ELECTRIC      6

3

HAND-CRANKED

1860      1870      1880      1890      1900      1910      1920

Albania
Argentina
Australia
Brazil
Bulgaria
Canada
Chile
China

Colombia
Denmark
Ecuador
Egypt
France
Greece
India
Indonesia
Iran
Israel
Italy
Japan
Libya
Netherlands
North Korea
Norway
Pakistan
Peru
Poland
Portugal
South Africa
Spain
Sweden
Taiwan
Turkey
UK
USA

USSR

Venezuela
West Germany
Yugoslavia

Conventional
Nuclear powered attack
Nuclear powered ballistic missile
Diesel powered ballistic missile

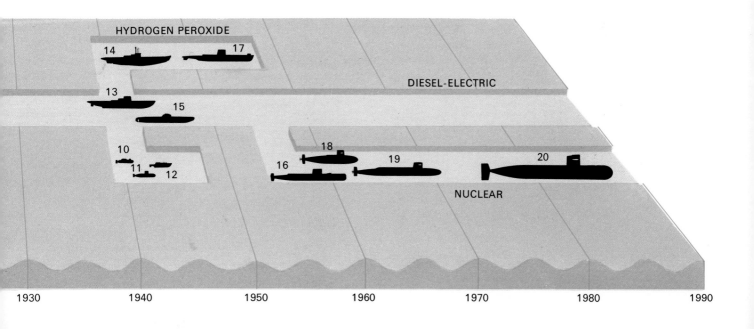

HYDROGEN PEROXIDE

DIESEL-ELECTRIC

NUCLEAR

14  17
13
15
10
11  12
18
16  19  20

1930    1940    1950    1960    1970    1980    1990

Above: The excellent US Mk 48 hunting torpedo. Below: Britain's inferior Tigerfish. Opposite: Launch of a SUBROC missile.

miles, a rather unsatisfactory distance.

*Invincible* is a particularly depressing example of another, specifically British, NATO weakness. This light carrier was laid down in 1973 but took four years to get into the water (launched May 1977) and was not commissioned until March 1980. Chronic labour problems in the dockyards and the appalling time taken to

complete essential overhauls remain the Royal Navy's biggest curse. In 1976 the frigate *Argonaut* went into dock to be refitted with the powerful French 'Exocet' SSM. Four years later she was still there.

Apart from its own numerical and internal weaknesses, NATO starts from an overriding fundamental disadvantage. NATO is a defensive alliance, and defensive alliances (as demonstrated in 1939–40) tend to have a disastrous 'first round' when attacked by a determined and well-armed single enemy. In terms of material the case of the American Mk 48 hunting torpedo may be cited. This, as mentioned above, is one of the most vital weapons in the NATO naval armoury, being the only operational weapon considered able to hit the new Soviet high-speed, deep-diving submarines. The Mk 48 has a speed of 50 knots and a range of 30 miles while its British equivalent, Tigerfish, is not only slower but has a minute range of $2\frac{1}{2}$ miles. Yet the British continue to decline American offers of the Mk 48, even when their American ally, in February 1980, offered Britain new manufacturing processes and £150 million worth of American orders if the Ministry of Defence would agree to the deal. This particular 'problem' of NATO, independent national weapons selection, is another acute weakness from which the Soviet Union and her satellites do not suffer.

In submarine ballistic missiles, NATO still preserves a dwindling lead over the Soviet Union, with 730 missiles carried in 45 submarines. The Soviet Union deploys 1028 missiles in 90 submarines—but this is nevertheless outclassed by the NATO superiority in MIRVed warheads. When the MIRV factor is added to present a comparative line-up of submarine-launched ballistic nuclear warheads, American and British combined forces emerge as clear potential winners with 5084 Polaris A-3 Poseidon C-3 warheads. Even taking the most generous view towards the Soviet MIRVing programme, this still leaves the Soviet Union with only 2516 warheads.

In nuclear attack submarines, Britain and the United States have a combined total of 83 ships to the Soviet Union's 41. But it is in conventional diesel-electric submarines, the veteran power plant of the two World Wars, that the most startling imbalance is revealed. The combined NATO diesel submarine strength, including Mediterranean members whose navies would hardly become involved in any imaginable naval conflict in the Atlantic, is no more than 109 boats. The Soviet Union has 138.

# 10. BLUEPRINT FOR WORLD WAR III

Previous page: The USA continues to build conventional-sized SSBNs such as the USS *Jackson*, here dwarfed by the first of a new generation of 16,000-ton Ohio-class ballistic missile boats.

Diesel-electric submarines have all but vanished from the US Navy's inventory, while retained by most NATO and some Warsaw Pact countries, including the USSR.

As mentioned in the last chapter, NATO pins its hopes on the likelihood of any full-scale Soviet attack being preceded by a period of increasing diplomatic tension and deteriorating relations. In naval terms this phase is traditionally accompanied by the aggressor sending his warships to their war stations before the outbreak of hostilities, as Germany did in August 1939. NATO's excellent surveillance systems are indeed well equipped to supply ample warning of such preparatory warship movements. But there is every chance that if the Soviet Union does decide to gamble on an all-out conventional war, her Navy will prepare for the conflict by doing precisely nothing, and keeping its shipping movements to their normal pattern. This surprising lack of Soviet naval activity on the eve of a major gamble—such as the invasion

of Czechoslovakia in 1968, or the mass air supply programme to Egypt and Syria during the Yom Kippur War of 1973—has twice caught the NATO planners by surprise. It could very well be employed again before The Day.

If this happens the best chance for the NATO Navies would be to move in hard and fast and seal off all the major exits which the Soviet Navy must command to reach the open seas: the Dardanelles in the Mediterranean, the Straits of Gibraltar, the Skagerrak and Kattegat at the mouth of the Baltic, and—widest and most difficult of all—the Greenland/Iceland/ United Kingdom gap. As the SSBNs move up to their optimum firing positions in the event of the nuclear threshold being crossed, the conventional diesel and nuclear hunter-killers will carry the weight of the battle. For the Soviet

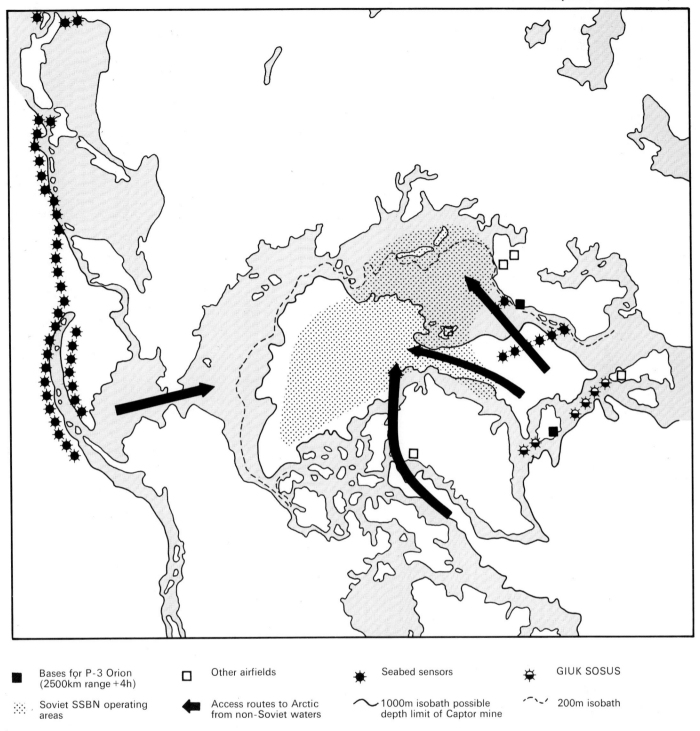

■ Bases for P-3 Orion
(2500km range +4h)

□ Other airfields

✴ Seabed sensors

✴ GIUK SOSUS

∷ Soviet SSBN operating
areas

◀ Access routes to Arctic
from non-Soviet waters

∿ 1000m isobath possible
depth limit of Captor mine

⌢ 200m isobath

submarine force has a third foe to be accounted for along with the SSBNs and Russian hunter-killers: cruise missile submarines, hangovers from the 1950s but armed with the 'Shaddock' anti-shipping missile. Should these break loose into the Atlantic, the task of the NATO forces might become all but impossible.

Defeat for NATO on the European continent, accomplished without resort to nuclear weapons, would be unlikely to leave Britain uninvaded. For the Soviet Navy, Britain's ports and naval bases would be objectives of the highest price, because the next phase would be the total isolation of the United States by the Soviet sub-

marine fleet. In a non-nuclear World War III, Britain would be invaded for precisely the same reason that Norway was invaded by Germany in April 1940: the strategic value of its coastline and ports.

One of the greatest mysteries of the postwar world is why the British—unlike the French—have lost all interest in conventional naval security. In the decade before World War II the British were acutely aware of the growing German threat in home waters; newspapers would heatedly debate every new addition to the German fleet, and demand assurances that the Royal Navy would be able to hold its own

Sensors covering the exits from, and the entry routes to the Soviet 'Sea Bastions' from which many of their ballistic missiles will be launched.

Specialists at work in the operations room of the Type 82 destroyer HMS *Bristol.* Some are tasked with the detection and destruction of enemy submarines.

in the event of war. But over the past 25 years Britain's journalists and broadcasters have shied away from sounding the tocsin.

Geography, however, has not changed since 1945. The British Isles remain the vital bridge across which supplies must be passed, in the event of war, to the NATO forces in Germany. The British Isles are also the crucial bastion for repelling any Soviet naval assault on the North Atlantic sealane. The weight of such an assault would be carried by the Soviet submarine fleet. It therefore follows that Britain *must* look to her conventional anti-submarine defences as a matter of the highest urgency. But there is little or no sign that this necessity is even recognised, let alone accepted, in Whitehall.

Instead, on 16 July 1980, the British Conservative government threw out its chest and announced the decision to adopt the Trident SLBM.

Ironically it was the *Daily Telegraph*, the only British newspaper faithfully to chart every addition to the Soviet fleet over the years, which waxed the most enthusiastic over the decision. The 'British element' of the project was proudly displayed:

'Britain is to build a new fleet of four nuclear submarines armed with the West's latest and most powerful missile—the American Trident, which will have British warheads.

The new force, a replacement for the Polaris in the mid-1990s, will cost £5000 million spread over the next 15 years. But over 70 percent of this sum will be spent in Britain and more than 200,000 jobs will be created in shipyards and component firms.'

Amid all the euphoria on one side and the ritual outrage of the unilateral nuclear disarmers on the other, *not one voice* was raised to ask how many Soviet warships could be sunk in a conventional naval war by Trident submarines. Nor, even more surprisingly, was there any attempt to challenge the decision by pointing out that if £5000 million was going to be spent on the Navy over the next 15-year period, it might be better to spend half that amount over the next *five* year period, to build warships and create jobs which are desperately needed now.

The Tactical command centre aboard *Le Redoubtable*, one of 6 such SSBNs representing France's truly independent nuclear deterrent.

Artist's impression of the Hawker Siddeley anti-shipping USGW (Underwater to Surface Guided Weapon) designed to be fired from a RN submarine's torpedo tubes. This system was dropped in favour of standardisation with the American Harpoon system.

This is not to affirm that Trident is an inferior weapon or a non-deterrent. On the contrary, it is the logical development of a system which has, as argued above, more than proved its worth for 20 crisis-ridden years. But there are higher priorities on which the money should be spent. NATO lacks sufficient surface naval forces to cope with the 'wild-goose' factor of undersea war. Time and time again during the Battle of the

Atlantic in World War II, over-stretched escorts took off in pursuit of promising contacts, leaving their charges to be savaged by U-boat packs. There is only one cure for this problem: have enough escorts to handle both the false alarms *and* the real source of the attack. In the 1980s NATO has an efficient if not perfect early-warning system, but not enough anti-submarine forces. Boasting about the excellence of NATO's

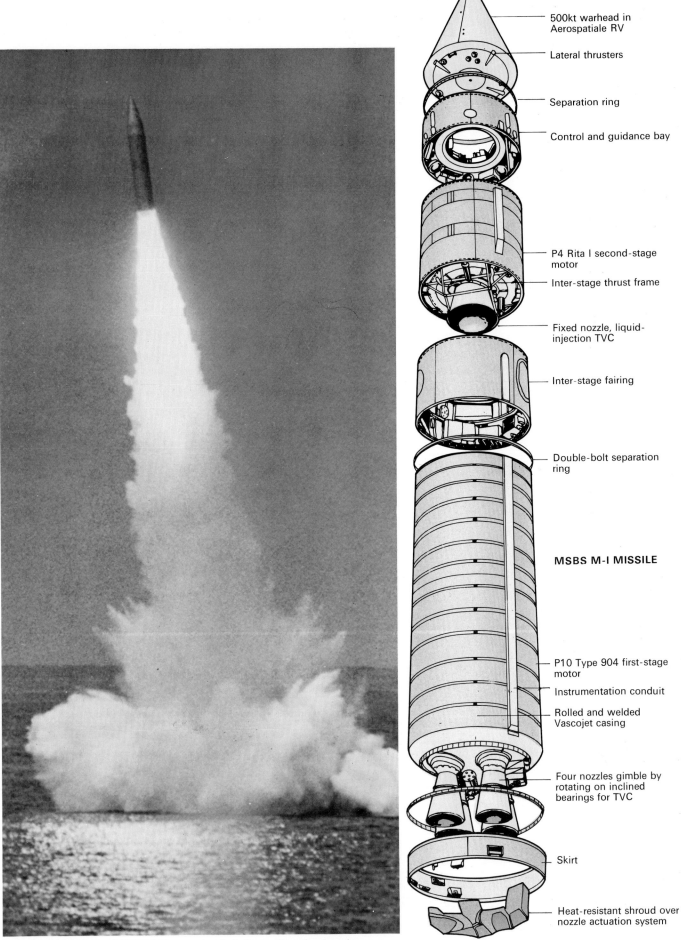

500kt warhead in
Aerospatiale RV

Lateral thrusters

Separation ring

Control and guidance bay

P4 Rita I second-stage
motor

Inter-stage thrust frame

Fixed nozzle, liquid-
injection TVC

Inter-stage fairing

Double-bolt separation
ring

**MSBS M-I MISSILE**

P10 Type 904 first-stage
motor

Instrumentation conduit

Rolled and welded
Vascojet casing

Four nozzles gimble by
rotating on inclined
bearings for TVC

Skirt

Heat-resistant shroud over
nozzle actuation system

Submerged launch of an MSBS M-20 strategic missile from a French submarine.

intelligence and technology is uncomfortably reminiscent of a man with the seat out of his trousers boasting about what a fine belt he has.

The Soviet Navy, on the other hand, has quite enough submarines with which to simulate a submarine breakout into the North Atlantic (as it has already done during NATO exercises), wait until the NATO surface forces have been redeployed to cope with this feint, then launch the main breakout force *en masse*.

An ominous indication of how threadbare NATO's anti-submarine forces have become is the Anglo-American 'Arapaho' project. This involves modifying container cargo ships to carry anti-submarine helicopters. Normal-sized cargo containers are used to house the helicopters, along with all their fuel, stores, workshop equipment, pilots and maintenance staff. The helicopters operate from a steel-mesh flight deck laid over the cargo containers. When, in time of war, the cargo ship so fitted arrived at its destination, the naval containers are unloaded first and added to the cargo of another outward-bound vessel.

Arapaho is, of course, nothing more than an updated rehash of the make-do 'Woolworth carriers' of World War II. They, too, were ordinary merchantmen modified to carry aircraft; they, too, were a frantic stop-gap introduced in dire emergency to atone for years of peacetime complacency and neglect. Details of Arapaho were published in April 1980—*along with the damning admission that the project had been 'under consideration' for the past ten years.* One is left speechless that such a basic deficiency could, in defiance of the lessons of two World Wars, be allowed to persist and intensify for a decade when it could have been remedied at a fraction of the cost of the Trident programme.

From these gloomy considerations it remains to conclude that the essentials of undersea war remain fundamentally unchanged in the 1980s. It may well be that an economically depressed Britain would be far better advised to pass the onus of strategic nuclear deterrence to her allies, and herself reassume the main burden of conventional anti-submarine defence in the eastern and north Atlantic. For improved technology and weaponry have not rendered obsolete the hydrophone, sonar, mine, torpedo, submarine-hunting aircraft-carrier, or diesel-electric submarine. And the fact that specialised submarines are now able to destroy civilian populations thousands of miles away has not deprived the submarine of its basic role: to sink enemy ships and deprive the enemy of free passage.

A huge underwater explosion follows the launch of an ASROC anti-submarine missile from the destroyer USS *Agerholm*. Such weapons, fitted with nuclear warheads, will probably be the first use of atomic weapons in World War III.

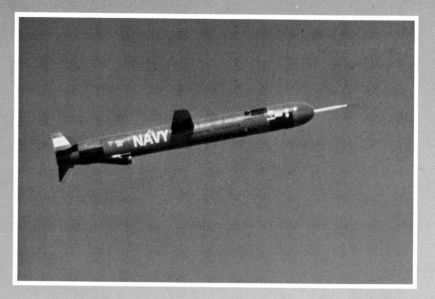

The US Navy's SLCM (Sea Launched Cruise Missile) bursts from the water during the second test firing of the missile. The BGM-109 Tomahawk is designed for launch from the torpedo tubes of a submerged submarine and is lifted to the surface by a booster which is then detached and the missile assumes the characteristic features of a low level, terrain matching cruise weapon with an ultimate range of 2,000 nautical miles.

# INDEX

# PICTURE CREDITS

The publisher would like to thank the following photographers, archives, illustrators and organisations who supplied material for this book. Illustrations are credited by page number. Where more than one photograph appears on a page, credit is given in the order of columns from left to right and then from top to bottom. Some sources have, for reasons of space alone, been abbreviated as follows:
Crown Copyright (Ministry of Defence-Royal Navy): MOD
Etablissement Cinematographique & Photographique des Armees: ECPA
Imperial War Museum, London: IWM
Military Archive & Research Services, London: MARS
US Navy Official Photo, Washington DC: USN
Prints of those illustrations marked with a * were supplied from MARS.

Front cover USN*; Dust jacket flap MARS; Endpapers USN*; 1–3 USN*; 4–5 IWM; 6–8 USN*; 8–9 MOD*; 10–11 Tekniska Museet, Stockholm*; 12–13 Royal Netherlands Navy*; 14–19 USN*; 20–21 MARS; 22–23 USN*; 23 MARS; 24–25 The Science Museum, London*; 25 (top) MARS; 25 (btm) The Science Museum, London*; 26 USN*; 26–27 The Submarine Museum, Groton*; 27–29 IWM; 31 Bildarchiv Preussischer Kulturbesitz; 32–33 Personality Pictures Library, London; 35 MARS; 36–37 IWM; 38–39 MARS; 40–41 Bildarchiv Preussischer Kulturbesitz; 42–49; 50–51 USN*; 51–52 IWM; 53 USN*; 54 Vickers Shipbuilding Ltd*; 54–56 (top) IWM; 56–57 Peter Cannings; 58–59 IWM; 60–61 USN*; 62 IWM; 63 (top) Peter Cannings; 63 (btm) IWM; 64 Personality Pictures Library; 65–67 Peter Cannings; 68 Bundesarchiv, Koblenz; 68–69 IWM; 70 Peter Cannings; 70–71 (top) Fox Photos, London; 70–71 (centre & btm) Nautic Presentations; 71 MARS; 72 Richard Natkiel; 73 IWM; 74–75 Fox Photos; 74–75 (insets) MARS; 76 IWM; 77 IWM*; 77 (btm) Richard Natkiel; 78–79 IWM; 80 Richard Natkiel; 81 (top) Nautic Presentations; 81 (btm) US National Archives*; 82–83 USN*; 84–85 IWM*; 86 Public Records Office; 87 (left) USN; 87 (right) IWM; 88–89 USN*; 89 (top) Peter Cannings; 90 (top) Peter Cannings; 90 (btm) IWM; 91–93 USN*; 94–95 IWM; 96–97 (top) USN*; 97 (centre & btm) Ann Ronan Pic. Lib.; 98 IWM; 99 IWM*; 100 IWM; 101 (top) USN*; 101 (btm)–102 IWM;

103–104 MARS; 105 IWM; 106–107 USN*; 108 IWM*; 109 USN*; 110–111 IWM*; 112–115 USN*; 117–118 Peter Cannings; 119 USN; 120–127 USN*; 128–130 MOD*; 130–131 B A Reeves; 132–133 Novosti Press Agency, London; 134–137 USN*; 138 Deutsches Museum, Munich; 138–139 USN; 141 (top) USN; 141 (btm) Lockheed Missile & Space Co; 142 (left) ECPA; 142 (right) Aerospatiale, Paris; 142–143 Aerospatiale; 144–147 MOD; 147 (btm) ECPA; 148 (top) General Dynamics—Electric Boat Division*; 148 (btm) USN*; 149 (left) USN*; 149 (btm right) General Dynamics; 150 Lockheed Missiles & Space Co*; 150–155 USN*; 156 (top) IWM; 156 (btm)–157 (top) MOD*; 157 (btm)–158 (top) USN*; 158 (btm) MOD*; 158–159 Peter Cannings; 160 (inset) MOD*; 160–163 USN*; 164 MOD*; 164–165 MOD*; 165 Associated Press Ltd, London; 166–169 USN*; 170–171 MOD*; 172–173 USN*; 173 MOD*; 174–175 Peter Cannings; 176 (top) USN*; 176 (btm) MOD*; 177 Goodyear Aerospace*; 178–180 USN*; 181 Richard Natkiel; 182 MOD*; 183 ECPA*; 184 British Aerospace—Missiles Group; 185 Aerospatiale*; 186–187 USN*; Back cover USN*.

## Author's Note

Readers are reminded that the newest warship specifications, strategic deployments, communications systems, etc, are constantly subject to modification as fresh details about them are released. The author wishes to point out that the most up-to-date specifications included in *Undersea Warfare* (particularly with regard to Chapters 7–10) have been quoted from the 1980–81 editions of *Jane's Fighting Ships* and *Weapon Systems* and *The Military Balance* (International Institute for Strategic Studies), up-dated with official press releases valid to mid-November 1980—the time of going to press.

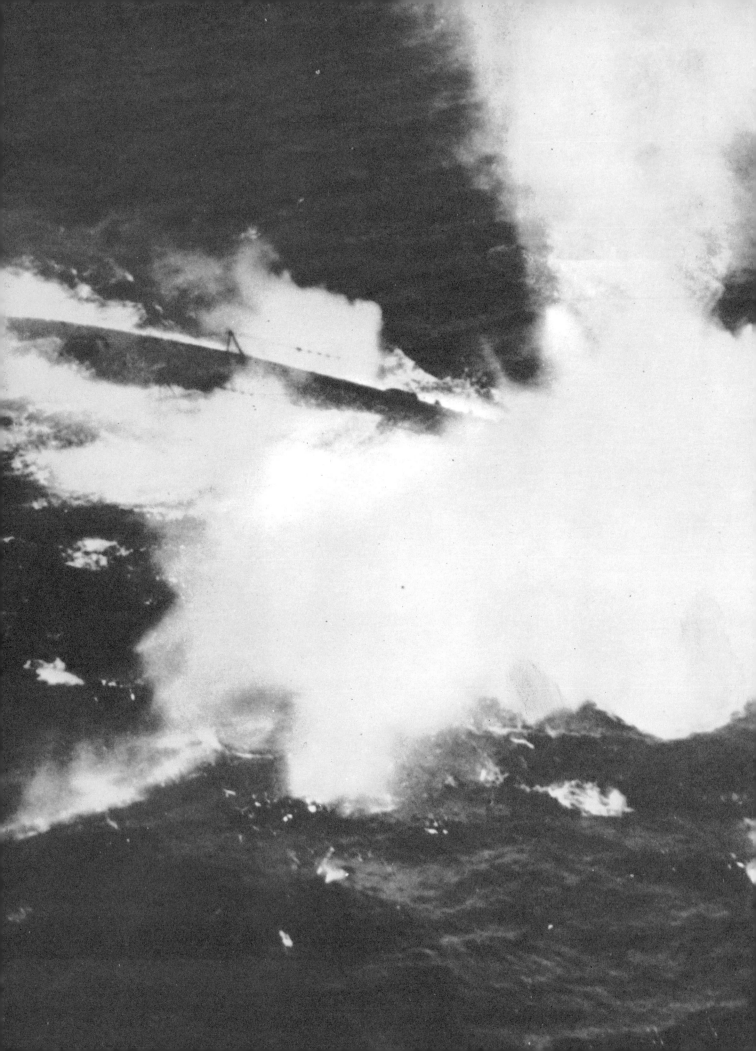